NOT JUST Pretty Face

One woman's riveting tale of survival

SHENITA JAMES

NOT JUST ANOTHER *Pretty Face*

One woman's riveting tale of survival

SHENITA JAMES

T&J PUBLISHERS

A SMALL INDEPENDENT PUBLISHER WITH A BIG VOICE

Printed in the United States of America by
T&J Publishers (Atlanta, GA.)
www.TandJPublishers.com

Cover Design by Timothy Flemming, Jr.
(T&J Publishers)
Book Format/Layout by Timothy Flemming, Jr.

ISBN: 978-1-7360003-5-9

To contact the author, go to:

www.IAmShenitaJames.com
JamesShenita@yahoo.com
Facebook: Shenita James
Instagram: Sheinta_James

To the memory of Dwayne Alex McCaskey, who was a wise counselor, one who was tender in heart, humble, and disciplined. You were so strong in your faith and purpose. I will always love you. I will never forget your words: "When proper preparation meets opportunity, take flight."

Dedications

First and foremost, I give honor to God for giving me the strength to overcome the obstacles I faced. I thank Him for His guidance and wisdom, and for allowing me to beat the odds and begin to walk in my purpose.

I would like to thank my mother, Claudia Council. I love you so much.

To my children, Ja'teria James, Jah-mel James, Jahquann Bulluck, and Jahquice James, thank you for all of your support and your words of encouragement during the process of me writing this book. I love you.

Secondly, I would like to thank Tammy Charity for encouraging me to continue to write during the most difficult times in my life.

I would to thank T&J publisher for making my dream a reality.

Lastly, to everyone who has supported and encouraged me to write my story from the beginning, I really appreciate you.

Table Of Contents

Chapter 1
A Girl's Dream

What a beautiful day it was. That morning, the sun shined radiantly upon our two-story brick house in the suburbs. I was busy chasing my brother up the stairs in a game of tag that morning. The smell of bacon and eggs filled the house while momma was in the kitchen. Daddy was sitting on the couch in the den, reading the morning paper. My big sister was in her bedroom with the door closed, doing whatever it was she'd be doing. My brother and I wouldn't dare enter into her room, or we'd receive a verbal thrashing. Usually, it was a thunderous "Get out of my room!" and "Shut my door!"

"Okay, everybody! Breakfast is ready!" mom yelled from the kitchen. Just then, my brother and I nearly tumbled down the stairs; our little footsteps thundered throughout the house like the sound of an earthquake as we raced to the kitchen. We hurried up and claimed our seats at the beautiful isle in the center of the kitchen. It matched the mahogany cabinets with granite counter-tops throughout the kitchen; this was complemented by the shiny, silver appliances—the refrigerator and built-in microwave sitting above the stove. Mom pulled a fresh batch of biscuits out of the large silver oven. The aroma was heavenly.

As mom placed the biscuits, eggs, bacon, and orange juice on the table, daddy grabbed her and pulled her close to himself. In their flirtatious way, mom leaned over and planted a big, juicy kiss on his lips, which prolonged longer than usual. My brother and I, blushing and in shock, covered our eyes and retorted the usual "Eew!" My sister, who came down from her lair looking like she'd just survived a zombie attack, just rolled her eyes.

"Do you two have to do that in front of us?" she asked, appearing flustered. But she could no longer conceal her smile beneath her hardened demeanor. She began to blush, as well. We all felt warm chills cascade all over us as mom and dad engaged in their little display of affection.

"Tina." I heard a voice calling. "Tina!" the person yelled. It was my mom. The sound of her voice snapped me out of my little fantasy, pulling me back into reality. It pulled me back into our small, wooden white house. It was a run-down little shack in a bad part of town. The white paint began to peel and wash away due to the wear and tear, dirt, and rain, causing the house to appear brown. Inside of the house, there was an old mothball smell combined with the smell of smoke from the kerosene heater. The inner walls had accumulated a build-up of dust and smut. We covered the windows with old blankets since we couldn't afford curtains. The floorboards would creak and crack whenever we walked on them.

There were four of us: me, my little brother, Roger, my big sister, Shasha, and my mom. My dad wasn't really in my life. As a little girl, I sensed that I was different from my siblings. My little mind wondered about things a small child shouldn't have to wonder about: *Why is life so painful? What is the purpose of life? Do I have a purpose?* Rather than my imagination soaring like an eagle into the stratosphere of some fantasy land with princes and dragons and elves and dwarfs, I fantasized about living what most people would consider a normal life. Out of all of my siblings, which actually consisted of three older siblings (two older siblings didn't live with us) and my younger brother, mom tended to show me more favoritism. Maybe it was because of my beautiful, slightly tanned skin; my thick, long hair; my dreamy eyes and pearly white smile. Perhaps, it was because of the way I made her feel by repeatedly telling her how much I loved her. Part of me believed it was because I reminded her of my dad, whom she loved dearly. Whatever the reason, she had no qualms with showing everyone in the household that I was her prized little possession, her treasure. She loved us all, but showed me special attention, and my siblings resented me for that.

We'd have special guests over at the house, but these were not the kind of guests anyone would want. At night, we'd share the bed with cockroaches, and we'd pray that they wouldn't crawl into our nostrils and ears while we slept.

The winter months were interesting. To keep us warm, mom would heat water and pour it into several empty milk jugs, and then place those jugs at our feet to generate some heat for us. Although she did her best, we could see in her eyes that the weight of poverty was wearing her down. Not having the basic things that the average American family possesses was stressful. She handled things the best way that she could, which may be why she stayed gone so much. Bingo was an escape for her. She'd leave us at home alone often, which forced Shasha to take care of my brother and me. She was just a teenager, but she had adult responsibilities.

We didn't have a stove, so Shasha had to cook whatever food we had on the kerosene heater. The heater smoked so badly that if we were to blow our noses, black smut would appear on the tissue. That little house was no place to live in. I was ashamed and embarrassed by how our house looked. I didn't want anyone, especially my friends, to come to our house. Whenever they'd ask to come over and play, I would make excuses to prevent them from coming. If they did come over, there would be nowhere for them to sit since we didn't own any furniture. There would be nothing to entertain them with since we didn't own a television. We barely had any food to eat. We didn't own any toys, and there were those uninvited guests who liked to make their presences known—scurrying across the squeaky floor, up the walls, and into the cracks and crevices of the house.

We weren't poor; we lived beneath the poverty line. And it was often that mom's voice had to snap me out of a dream and pull me back into this reality. At one point, she wondered if I was losing my hearing—she'd be calling my name, but I wouldn't hear her. I was lost in a fairytale of a big, brick house with furniture, a television, essential appliances, one that was pest-free and filled with love. I dreamed of a father wrapping his strong arms around me and affirming me as his little girl. That was probably the biggest element of my fantasy life. I wanted to be able to curl up on the couch in front of the television with my two siblings and two loving parents with a bowl of popcorn more than anything.

A Prayer Answered

And I was ready and willing to settle for anything that resembled my fantasy world. I wanted a father. I wanted to be able to enjoy family rituals that bonded us together. I wanted a home I could be proud of. I'd pray and ask God for these things. And it didn't take long for an answer to my prayers to come. Mom finally found love again. His name was Jeffery.

One of the distinguishing characteristics of Jeffery was his smell. He reeked of Old Spice cologne. We could have dubbed him the Old Spice man and placed him in the commercials. He was a big man, standing at 6'3. He was slim and handsome. He had the most beautiful eyes; they were green. He was caramel-complexioned and loved to tote a big, perfectly shaped afro. He certainly had charm, and it was easy to see why mom was so captivated by him. He was the answer to my prayers. He had to be. He'd dashed into our lives like a rushing wind and filled in the gaps in my little heart.

Mom was still spending time away from us, but this time, she wasn't at the bingo hall; she was with Jeffery; they were growing closer and closer, while, in the meantime, life was continuing as usual for my siblings and me. We were still battling the cockroaches at night, who seemed to grow bolder and more aggressive. I guess they began to consider themselves a part of the family. We were still seeking after ways to overcome the cold. Our stomachs were still growling and filled with hunger pains. But we could see a subtle difference. Mom glowed more, and Jeffery began to load us with gifts. He stepped in and lent us help and support, which was invaluable in our struggle to survive. Upon seeing our living condition, he was appalled and made us an offer that was difficult to refuse: he asked us to move in with him. I was ecstatic! At least a part of my dream was coming true. Anything better than our little roach-motel would be significantly better. When Jeffery asked mom to move in with him, I imagined him having a big house filled with furniture, a television, appliances, one that was spacious with a big backyard so me and Roger could run until our little hearts' were content. Of course, that's not what we got. His place was different from what I expected. Very different.

My siblings and I were shocked when we arrived at his house. It was like entering another dimension as if we were living in The Twighlight Zone. *Where the heck are we?* I thought—the property reeked with the smell of hog manure. Chickens were running wild all over the place. There was a vegetable garden in the front yard. I'd never seen anything like this being from the city. *So this is what they call the country.*

Jeffery's house wasn't much. It was a small, blue, rusted mobile home with a porch. Inside the house, it was tight. The living room smelled like Marlboro cigarettes. It had three mix-matched chairs that had holes in them, a television that only played three channels, and an ironwood heater that dusted the room with ashes. The walls had yellow floral pattern wallpaper on them. My bedroom was so tiny it could only fit a bunk bed. To enter the bedroom, we had to turn sideways. The bathroom had a light blue sink, and we had to use pliers to turn the water on and off. The toilet did not flush, and the tub was there for decoration; it didn't work. To bathe, we had to go outside to the water pump and fill-up five-gallon buckets. We had to fill these buckets with water and use it to flush the toilet as well.

Despite everything I'd just mentioned about Jeffery's house, we made it home. My overactive imagination was able to gloss over it and turn it into a mansion in my mind. The best part was we had fun, so much fun. Although the television only played three channels, it was a dream come true to huddle up with my family and the man who had stepped in to become a father-figure and watch television together; this is what I'd always dreamed of; it's what I always wanted. I was beginning to experience what most people call normalcy.

Living with Jeffery was a unique experience; it was like having a zoo in our front yard. Jeffery taught us how to feed the hogs and chickens, which was a lot of fun. Me and Roger found it fascinating when the animals would run up to us when it was feeding time. Jeffery took my siblings and me fishing, which was something new to me. He showed us how to take care of a garden—how to pull up weeds and water it. Sure, we didn't have a traditional household, but we had each other, and we appreciated what we had. In a sense, we had a complete family, and I couldn't have been happier. Life was good... for now.

Chapter 2
The Nightmare Begins

Months had gone by, and the newness of being in a new house was wearing off. We had grown used to the chickens and hogs, and the garden felt more like hard labor rather than a fun exercise. For mom, the lure of a new love began to wear off also. She and Jeffery were a thing now; they were a couple; and like many couples, routine habits started to slip to the forefront. Mom's old habits resurfaced. Once again, she started leaving the house for long periods of time to indulge in bingo marathons, leaving us alone to be supervised by Shasha. However, this time, we weren't alone—Jeffery was there.

Let's Play A Game

Mom left the house every day like clockwork, which didn't seem to bother Jeffery; he'd grown used to it. With time, he began to encourage mom to go to her bingo sessions. He'd willingly drop her off and give her money. At times, he seemed a little too happy to see her go; after all, that's what she enjoyed doing. While she was gone, he found other things to do around the house.

Upon returning home after he'd drop mom off, Jeffery would slip into a relaxed state and focus his attention on us. He enjoyed playing with us, especially with Shasha. One of his favorite things to do with her was play a game he called "Ride The Horse" where he'd have her bounce up and down on his lap. This looked like so much fun. My sister would be laughing, smiling, and she appeared to be having the time of her life, which made me envious. So I'd run up to Jeffery and scream, "Do me! I'm next!" While playing this game with him, I'd laugh so hard my stomach would ache and tears would stream down my eyes. These were tears of joy, tears every little girl longs to cry while basking in the warmth, love, and affection of a father; this was the most fun I'd ever had.

One day, after we finished playing Ride The Horse, Jeffrey called Shasha into his bedroom and insisted that me and Roger remain in the living room. He put a movie in the VCR, gave us some cookies, and told us not to get up for anything until he told us to do so. I didn't think anything of it, that is, until me and Roger heard strange creaking sounds coming from the bedroom. Curious, I wanted to know what the noises were. I tipped toed down the hallway to the bedroom to listen closely. I gently placed my ear to the bedroom door. Shasha was making strange noises—moaning sounds. I heard Jeffery murmuring, "It was good." *What is good?* I wondered. "Do not tell anyone about this, and I promise I will always be good to you," Jeffrey said to her. My eyes dilated, and my mouth dropped open. I was shocked. I then rushed back into the living room and sat next to Roger. I leaned over and whispered to him,

"I think they are doing the nasty."

"Yuck, that is gross," he replied.

"I'm telling mommy!" I exclaimed. When mom got home, I ran to tell her about the noises that Shasha made while she was alone with Jeffery. She told me to be quiet and go sit down. "But mommy!"

"Now!" she yelled. She refused to listen to anything I had to say.

I thought about the day my mom revealed to my grandfather that she was about to move in with Jeffery. While she was packing our things, which was not much, my grandfather pleaded with her to reconsider moving in with Jeffery, and he asked her not to move us into Jeffery's place. He knew something we didn't know about Jeffery. Jeffery had a reputation in the community that preceded him. Granddaddy knew we were heading for destruction. He warned mom that the man she was about to move in with was known for being involved with the mother and daughter at the same time. I don't think his words ever registered with her. All she cared about was she'd finally found someone to love her, and that could provide a stable place for her children to live.

Jeffery and Shasha continued their daily routine, going to the bedroom after mom left. He was confident my mother would not believe me. He no longer tried to hide his relationship with my sister. He started grabbing her butt and kissing her in the mouth in front of us. Me and Roger told mom what was going on. She finally confronted the two of them and asked them if our allegations were true. They denied everything though. After that, things began to go from bad to worst. What started out as a happy home filled with love and laughter turned into a home filled with betrayal and deceit. To make matters worse, my mom did not see any of it.

While me and Roger were trying to get mom to see the truth about Jeffery, Jeffery was busy attempting to turn us against our mom. He tried to brainwash us by telling us horrible things about her, saying, "She does not love you. All she cares about is bingo, and herself." He'd wait until she left to give us his little talks. Immediately after talking to us, he'd make us go to bed. Sometimes, the sun was still up. I tried to convince my brother the things Jeffery said about her were not true. But when I looked into his eyes, I saw the hurt and pain he was feeling. I was starting to feel it myself. I began wondering whether or not he was telling the truth about my mother.

The Assault

One night, while I was taking a bath, Jeffery came into the bathroom. I quickly put both of my hands in front of me to cover my body parts. He stood there for a moment, lustfully staring at me. "Pardon me, I didn't know anyone was in here," he said with a mischievous grin on his face. The way he looked at me gave me goosebumps. Later, while everyone was asleep, he entered into my bedroom—me and Roger slept in bunk beds. I jumped once I saw him. I was still bothered by the way he looked at me earlier, and I knew what he planned to do. He put his index finger over his mouth, signaling for me to keep quiet. As he came closer, he knelt beside my bed and whispered, "It's okay. Don't be afraid. I promise it will not hurt, nor will it take long." I was shaking because I had witnessed him touch my sister in places I knew were private. I knew he was about to touch me the same way. He gently put his hand on my face and whispered, "Just relax." He then pulled the covers back and rubbed his giant hand on my vaginal area and my small breasts, then he took things even further.

That was the moment my life was turned upside down. I was only seven-years-old at the time. I did not know what hurt the most: the assault or the betrayal. I loved him. He was like a father to me. I thought he loved me, too. He was so nice to me, and he did fun things with me. But now, I laid there helplessly; my tears flooding my pillow. I wanted to scream for my mom, but I had no vocals. I tried to move, but I felt paralyzed. I kept my eyes closed the entire time, hoping everything was a nightmare. When he was done, he whispered in my ear not to tell anyone. His warm breath sent chills all over my body, but his words went in one ear and out the other. He told me that even if I did tell someone, they would not believe me and that my mom would give me a spanking. After that, he left the room, but his Old Spice cologne lingered behind.

I lied there in fear, wondering if he was going to return. Once I realized he was long gone, I climbed to the top bed with Roger, and we held each other tight. Although my little brother never confessed to me that he knew what took place, I felt he sensed something was wrong because he cried as he consoled me. The next morning, I sat on the floor next to my mom's bedroom. When she opened the door, I wanted her to notice me—noticing that something was wrong with me—and ask me, "Are you okay?" I wanted her to see the hurt and pain in my eyes. But she just looked at me and ordered, "Get up off the floor." I slowly got up from the floor and walked away. I thought about how I would articulate what Jeffery had done to me, but I chose to keep silent. I was afraid and feeling lost. I did not know what to do or what to think. All I knew was what Jeffery did was wrong. I hated what was happening to me. But as a child, I'd been made to feel as if I had no voice. I was afraid to speak out. Still, I continued to pray that someone would notice me and save me from Jeffery.

What I first thought was a blessing turned out to be a curse. Jeffery was no father-figure; he was a predator. I learned that sometimes the devil will send a counterfeit answer to our prayers.

August 1987

We returned to school from our summer break. The children were happy and boasted about the wonderful things they had done over the summer. My mind wandered off, recalling the horrible events that took place at Jeffery's house. "Shenita, what did you do while you were on break?" the teacher asked. My thoughts were racing, and my heart skipped a beat. I so badly wanted to burst out in tears. *Oh, my God! What do I say?* I was trying to think of something to say quick before my eyes welled up with tears.

"Look at that bug!" I yelled suddenly, diverting the attention away from me. I was anxious for school to end. I glanced at the clock on the wall nearly every thirty minutes to see if it was time to get on the bus. I was ready to go home and be with my mother. I wanted her to realize that something was wrong with her daughter. I sat at my desk all day, drawing pictures of a mean, ugly monster that reminded me of Jeffery. I was angry; furious. I raised my pencil to stab the monster in the face, but the bell rang. *Ah, the moment I'd waited for all day!*

Before then, I loved going to school; now, I preferred to stay at home with my mom. I cried every night and thought about ways that I could stay home with her. I pretended to be sick so she would not leave me alone with *him.* I wanted her to know that her innocent daughter had a dark secret. Whenever I thought about telling her what Jeffery did to me, I remembered that she did not believe me and Roger when we told her about what Jeffery was doing with Shasha. I had so many thoughts going through my mind: *What if my mom punishes me? What if my mom believes me?* I was hurting, and I did not know what to do or whom to trust.

Eventually, I told mom, and to my surprise, she

believed me. She said not to tell anyone and promised me that she would look for another place for us to live. I promised not to tell anyone about what Jeffery was doing to me, feeling optimistic. However, that feeling of hope began to fade as mom turned her attention to bingo and continued to leave us home alone with Jeffery, who continued to abuse me. Mom knew he was hurting her daughters. As I got older, I tried to make sense of it all, and wondered if she was in shock, in denial, or simply blinded by love.

Shasha was falling in love with Jeffery before my mother's very eyes. She wrote *"Shasha loves Jeffrey, always and forever"* on her skin and on all of her notebooks, and drew hearts around it. She was in the eighth grade at the time. There were plenty of times when, during class, my sister would skip school and walk to his job, which was not far. She would sit in his car until it was time for him to get off of work. The principal called my mom and informed her of my sister's absences. Mom was distraught after hearing this. She just knew Shasha was in school. She watched her get on the school bus. When mom confronted her about skipping school, Shasha started to mouth-off at her. And before I knew it, mom slapped her across the face; that's when the fight started. Me and Roger were in a state of shock, afraid, watching, crying, and yelling, "Stop! Get off of my mommy!" Jeffery finally intervened and pulled the two of them apart. He told mom that it was her fault, not Shasha's. She then looked up at him with tears in her eyes and left out of the house. She left us alone with Jeffery again.

CHAPTER 2: THE NIGHTMARE BEGINS

Roger asked me, "Why does mommy leave us alone? Is she upset with us, too?" I couldn't provide him with an answer. I was terrified, and mentally drained. I worried about my mom, wondering where she could be. She was hurting. That night, me and Roger were sent to bed after eating only a can of Great Northern Beans seasoned with smoked pig meat. I prayed and asked God to make my mother come back home earlier, but it seemed as if my prayer was in vain.

No child should have to witness his or her mother and sister physically fight each other. Although the fight was between them, my brother and I felt like the burden was resting on our shoulders. We were traumatized, and left alone to deal with the effects.

NOT JUST ANOTHER PRETTY FACE

Chapter 3

Signs

Jeffery continued to come into my bedroom night after night while everyone was asleep. He would pull back the covers and repeat his routine. His moans and the sensation of his hot breath on my skin made me feel sick. After he finished, he would always tell me how good it felt. Sometimes, he would put his hands on my face and say, "You are so beautiful and special to me." As always, I could not stop crying. I could hear my heart beating. I felt confused. What really confused me was when he said he loved me. I couldn't understand how love could make someone feel so bad. If he loved me, why did he keep hurting me?

Furthermore, my mom told me she loved me, but she never stayed home with me. She'd abandon us, leaving us to suffer at the hands of a monster to enjoy a game of bingo. Was bingo more important than us? Was love supposed to look and feel like this?

My heart was weighed down by a ton of worries. My hope for a brighter day was slowly fading. I was desperate to stop Jeffery from hurting me. The next morning, when mom got us up for school, I went into the bathroom and began crying uncontrollably; the graphic events of the night before continued to play in my mind. "I hate him! I hate him!" I yelled repeatedly as I punched myself in the nose. My nose started to bleed profusely. I was so upset, I did not notice the amount of blood that had poured from my nose. I started to feel light-headed, dizzy, and afraid. I could not stop the blood from flowing. I yelled for mom to come and help me. She rushed into the bathroom.

"What happened?" she asked.

"I don't know, mommy. My head hurts really bad, and my nose will not stop bleeding," I answered. Mom placed a cold rag over my head and a brown piece of paper on my upper lip, then she told me to hold my head back until the bleeding stopped.

"You are not going to school today," she said. She decided to let me hang out with her for the day, which filled my heart with so much joy. So after everyone left the house, the two of us went to the city. I was happy that I had her full attention. We ate breakfast and lunch together. We visited my grandparents' house. I was having so much fun, that is, until it was time to head back home. Mom had to hurry back to get Roger off the bus. The closer we got to the house, the faster my heart beat. My breaths grew short. As I stared out of the car window, everything suddenly became a blur. My head began to spin. I felt nauseous, sick, and terribly confused, not knowing what was going on with me. I dropped my doll baby onto the seat and began hyperventilating. The only thing playing in my mind was the recollection of the horrible events that occurred the night before. Mom noticed how sick I looked, and instructed me to lie down and get some rest once we got home. Her motherly care and affection were so comforting, soothing, and reassuring, I didn't want her to leave. I just wanted her to stay with me, to comfort me and let me know everything was going to be alright. My heart ached for her presence, but deep in my heart, I knew she would be preparing to leave soon. I was desperate to make her stay home, so I made my nose bleed again. I allowed the blood to pour freely until my face, shirt, and hands were covered in it. I held my head back so the blood would stop pouring from my nose, but then thick clots of blood came from my mouth. I spat the clotted blood onto my hands and then shouted frantically,

"Mommy, look!" She rushed into the bedroom, and after seeing me, rushed me to the hospital. The doctor told her not to worry and said I'd either gotten too hot or too excited. He instructed her to keep a close eye on me, which she did. She didn't allow me to go to school for the remainder of the week. She called my dad and informed him of my nose bleeds. He suggested that I stay with him and his girlfriend while I was out of school. Mom agreed. I felt safe while I was at my dad's house. No one there tried to hurt me. I was able to be a child. I felt loved. My dad's girlfriend braided my hair into two braids with a part down the middle with pink and white barrettes at the end. She dressed me in a hot pink floral dress and a pair of clear jelly sandals. For a moment, I felt like I was back in one of my dreams, one of my fantasies. I was experiencing the bliss of a loving family, the paradise of love, safety, and security. And then, I heard a knock at the door. It was my mom. She was there to pick me up and take me back to the reality I deeply hated. She was there to take me back to Jeffery. I dreaded going back there. I took my time packing my bag, trying to prolong the time as much as possible. I was trying to figure out a way to avoid going back there, so I hid my shoes, hoping my mom would say I could stay another night with my dad. But that didn't work. She insisted that I leave and go back with her even without any shoes on. Even seeing the tears in my eyes as she said it, she was unrelenting, determined to take me back to a living Hell.

Backfired

Jeffery and Shasha would go out of town often to sell hogs; they'd leave my mom behind. When they returned, he had what appeared to be a lot of money. He always took good care of my sister. He made sure she got whatever she wanted. He'd bring food home and place it inside of the freezer in the barn. Only he and Shasha had keys to the freezer. My mom had to get my sister's permission to retrieve food out of the freezer to cook. When Fridays came, Jeffery took Shasha to the city, and they would order carry-out from a fast food restaurant called "Little Man". They served delicious double cheese-burgers and crispy brown French fries. Meanwhile, my brother and I ate Ramen Noodles and ham sandwiches.

Shasha had everything: money, plenty of snacks, and games. I hated her and Jeffery for the Hell they were putting the rest of us through. Me and Roger only had each other. What hurt me the most was my mother saw what this man was doing, but she wouldn't stop it; she wouldn't stand up for us and protect us. On the days my mom did decide to stay home from bingo, Shasha would lie on the bathroom floor next to mom's bedroom and eavesdrop on her and Jeffery's conversations. Whenever mom told her to stop eavesdropping and go to bed, they would end up fighting.

Roger and I grew used to this routine. Once the yelling started, we'd climb into the bed together and cry while holding each other tight. "I love you," I'd tell him.

"I love you, too," he'd reply. Moments later, we'd be sound asleep.

As time progressed, the trauma of sexual and psychological abuse began to wear on me and my siblings even more. We were manifesting signs of abuse in various ways. It felt like a tornado ripped our family apart. Before Jeffery came into our lives, we were poor, but we were together; now we had more, but we were no longer together. And truth be told, we didn't have that much more than Jeffery to begin with. It's not like living with him was a huge step up from our poverty-stricken life in the city.

Shasha started abusing herself by cutting her

body with glass. Roger started wetting the bed at night. I began experiencing anxiety and panic attacks like the one I experienced in the car coming from my dad's house. Of course, mom saw the red flags. She had to. They were impossible to miss. How could she not see there was something wrong with her children? And yet, she pretended like there was nothing wrong.

We were kids. We were being abused and didn't know how to communicate what was happening to us. We shouldn't have had to look for ways to explain to her what was obvious. As a parent, she should have noticed the subtle changes in our behavior and detected that there was something off with us. Rather than fleeing to the bingo hall, we hoped she would focus on us and seek to discover why we were acting so strangely. Why were we having fits of rage, wetting the bed, having panic attacks, crying suddenly, and hyperventilating upon arriving at Jeffery's house? We just wanted her attention and concern. That's all.

Chapter 4

Voodoo

It was a cold night in December. The wind was blowing; snow covered the ground. I can remember that night like it was yesterday. Jeffery got out of bed to put more wood inside of the heater so it would burn all night. I trained myself to sleep light. I wanted to hear the floor squeak when he got up so that I could prepare for what was about to take place. That night, he crept into my bedroom and violated me as he usually did, but this time, he used his mouth. My legs quivered, my stomach fluttered, my heart pounded, and my tears fell uncontrollably. While he was assaulting me, I was praying that someone would come in and witness the gruesome things he was doing to me, but no one did. My silent plea was that my mother would walk in and save me. When he finished, he wiped my tears, told me he loved me, and then gave me a ten-dollar bill.

As a child, I did not realize this psychopath was

paying me "hush money" to keep me quiet about his molesting me. He was teaching me that it is okay to get raped as long as you receive some payment. I was so angry I wanted to stick a knife into his heart and watch the blood drain out of him. Instead, I balled the money up and climbed onto the top bunk with my little brother. I held my brother tight, and I cried, wondered if this pain would ever leave.

The next morning, when my mom woke me and Roger up for school, we were drenched in urine. Roger wet the bed. He knew Jeffery was hurting me, but he felt powerless in that there was nothing he could do to help me. But each night, he went to bed with the same fear and anxiety that gripped me. After discovering that my brother wet the bed, mom became furious. She told me to go outside and get her two switches so she could beat him. I wanted to tell her, no, but I was too afraid. I was heartbroken and angry. Reluctantly, I went outside and picked the smallest switches I could find. I didn't want the switches to hurt him. While my mom was whooping him, I cried as if she was whooping me.

That morning, at school, I was full of anger and hatred. I replayed in my mind the whooping mom gave my brother and the things Jeffery did to me the night before. I tried to disguise my feelings while I was in school, laughing, playing, and joking with the other children. However, my teacher saw past my smile. She pulled me to the side and asked if I was okay. My heart skipped a beat. I wanted to say "no," but I lied and said "yes." How I managed to avoid bursting into tears while in school that day was beyond me.

When my brother and I came home from school, we smelled the aroma of food on the porch. Mom was cooking great-northern beans, frying pork chops, and baking biscuits from scratch. My mouth watered as I waited to dip my biscuit into some molasses. Mom told us to have a seat at the table so that we could eat. On our plates were beans and a biscuit. I asked my mom, "Where is the meat?" She jokingly responded,

"Run around the house and see who I meet!" Jeffrey and Shasha had crispy brown pork chops on their plates. I pouted and started to cry.

"I hate this house! I hate staying here! I wish I was dead!" I yelled.

"Look at me, and wipe your face right now! You better be thankful you are eating that!" Mom responded. My nose was running, and tears were streaming down my cheeks. When no one was looking, I spit the beans into my hands, and then poured the juice on my arms.

"Mommy! Look!" I beckoned.

"What happened to you?"

"I don't know. My food just started to come back out!" I noticed that pretending to be sick was the best way to get my mom's full attention.

Mom rushed me to the hospital. The doctor referred me to a specialist who ordered different lab tests. Although some of the tests were painful, I preferred to be stuck with needles rather than have Jeffery molest me. I still have scars on my body from some of the tests the doctors performed on me, but none of those scars can compare to the scars Jeffery left on my soul. Neither the doctors nor the specialists could understand why my food wasn't staying down. After months of observation, they told my mom there was nothing more they could do for me. One doctor even suggested that she seek spiritual guidance in this matter.

Mom was trying to figure out what was wrong with me; this was odd because, deep down inside, I suspected she knew but was unwilling to accept the truth. Remember, she had acknowledged earlier that she knew Jeffery was abusing me, and yet, she refused to protect us and get us out of Jeffery's house. She would continue to leave us at home alone with a monster. She was also being abused but decided to accept the unacceptable. She chose to allow Jeffery and his lover, her daughter, to trample on her. When a person doesn't possess a healthy sense of self-respect, they'll let others stomp on them. In my case, it took me years to discover that mom couldn't help me because she couldn't help herself. She was willing to take every route but the right one, and do everything but the right thing because she was afraid to face her demons. And speaking of demons . . .

The House of Horrors

Mom took the doctor's advice and sought spiritual counsel, but this was not the type of counsel I expected. She took me to a warlock, which is a male witch. This man specialized in "reverse spells." When we drove up to his place, I was terrified. It was an old, rusted, white trailer trimmed with yellow boarding. It looked like it belonged in a horror movie. From inside the car, I could smell the mothballs he put down around the house. He later explained to us that they were there to keep away "the evil spirits."

I reluctantly got out of the car. As we got closer to the steps to enter into the dark, gloomy house, a short, brown complexioned old man came out to greet us. He had a ball head, glossy popped eyes, and giant hands. When he reached for my hand, I grabbed my mom, hid my face with her pants, and held onto her leg tightly. I did not want to go with the creepy old man. I thought he was the devil. Both he and mom assured me that I was safe and that he was only going to "heal" me of whatever it was that was afflicting me.

Trusting my mom, I slowly let go of her leg and eased towards him. I extended my hand, and he shook it. Inside of the house, candles were burning everywhere, at every window and table. He had an outdated record player that played opera music. I glanced around in fear and continuously jumped whenever the music changed tone, going from a low to a high pitch. I sat at the table with the old man. He sat a white crystal ball, some oil, and a Bible on the table.

He rubbed some oil in the palm of my hand and started speaking in another language. I was frightened, unsure of what he was doing to me. I looked at my mom to see if she was going to intervene and save me. Tears were rolling down both of our faces, but she refused to step in and stop the ceremony the old man was performing over me. After a few minutes, the old man stopped and told my mom someone had placed "roots" on me to get back at her. He continued to mumble incoherently and occasionally read a scripture from the Bible. I had goosebumps all over my body as he spoke. Finally, he gave my mom a brown bag filled with different crafted dolls, oil, and body wash that smelled awful. He gave her precise instructions and told her to follow them exactly as stated. One set of instructions stood out to me: We had to go to a graveyard at midnight to collect some dust to put in my bathwater, along with the body wash I used every night. Me going to a place where the dead rests was inexplicable! There is no way she is going to make me go!

After we left the "Haunted House," my mom became convinced in her mind that the person "working roots" on me was my dad's girlfriend. Mom didn't like her because of my dad, so she blamed her for hurting me. She told everyone my dad's girlfriend put roots on me. I felt anxious and disturbed while hearing mom tell people that because I knew my dad's girlfriend loved me, and I loved her, and she would never do anything to hurt me. I stopped by my dad's house to see his girlfriend. When she opened the door, I knew someone had already called her with the bad news! Tears filled her eyes as she informed me that I was no longer welcomed there because of the terrible allegations my mom had made against her. She assured me that she would never do anything to hurt me; that very moment, I wanted to tell the truth, but I couldn't. I asked her for a hug.

"I am sorry baby," she said heartbroken before

closing the door in my face. My heart was crushed. Tears fell from my eyes. I instantly felt alone, empty, and bitter within.

"Why?! Why?! Why?!" I cried as I turned and walked away. Although I longed for my mom's attention and hoped she would rescue me from Jeffery, I never imagined I would have the attention of the community placed on me. Nothing could have prepared me for the embarrassment I was about to experience.

NOT JUST ANOTHER PRETTY FACE

Chapter 5

Finding Hope

My aunt told my mom about a lady that could help me. Her name was Hope. My mom called her on the telephone and told her about my "illness." She was excited about meeting me. She was single, and she loved children—she did not have any of her own. Hope suggested that I go to church with her and have her pastor pray for me. The following Sunday, she arrived at my house around 9 am. She was dark-complexioned with black curly hair. She wore a long purple blazer, a flashy button-up white blouse, a purple skirt trimmed in white, and a pair of black wedge heels. She smelled like a sweet flower. I ran and gave her the tightest hug as if I had known her all of my life. I jumped in her car, fastened my seatbelt excitedly, and then waved goodbye to my mom as we drove off.

When we arrived at the church, people were singing and clapping. The preacher asked me to come to him for prayer. It took me forever to walk the short distance from my pew to the altar. I was nervous because people were staring at me; they were whispering to one another. I could hear some of them saying, "That's the little girl that is sick." Some of the people believed based on rumors that I was demon-possessed. When I finally made it to the altar, the preacher explained to me the importance of accepting Jesus Christ as my Lord and Savior.

"Jesus will be with you forever. His Holy Spirit will protect you from evil, and you will have eternal life," he said. Most of what he said sounded like a foreign language to me, except for one part: the one where he said, "His Holy Spirit will protect you from evil." When he said those words, I thought about the evil I needed protection from - Jeffery. If this Holy Spirit will protect me from Jeffery, then I'm in, I thought.

Immediately, I shouted, "Yes!" I wanted Jesus and His protection from the monster haunting my bedroom at night. The preacher prayed with me to accept Christ as my Lord and Savior. After the prayer, I turned to walk back to my seat. Just then, the preacher called me up again, this time with a word of prophecy for me.

"Young girl, you are very special, and one day you will spread the gospel of Jesus Christ." I did not know what he meant, but at that moment, I felt relieved knowing God had a plan for me. I began to run and shout aloud "I am a winner!"

Even after church service was over, I was running over with excitement. While getting in the car, I was thinking to myself, I cannot wait to get home. I couldn't wait to tell my mom the good news. When I got home, I jumped out of the car and ran to my mom. "Mommy! Mommy! Guess what the preacher told me! He said "'I was special, and one day I am going to be like Jesus!"

"That is right, baby, you are very special," mom replied. However, she didn't seem very excited. There was a look of worry in her eyes. She then turned to Hope and asked her if the members of the church could buy us some food because we didn't have anything in the house to eat. Before Hope could answer, I was pulling on mom's skirt to ask her if I could stay with Hope. Mom didn't answer right then; she just told me to go inside and change my clothes. She and Hope stayed outside talking for a while. Finally, Hope left, and mom came back inside. She then asked me if I had told anyone about what was going on in our house. "No, mommy," I answered.

"That is right, baby. What goes on in my house stays in my house." Her expression was stern. Hope returned from the store with several bags filled with food. I was astonished by all of the bags. I peeped inside and then celebrated, "Yes!" For once, there were no Ramen Noodles or hot-dogs. "All this food! My brother and I are going to eat some good food tonight," I said to myself.

After dropping off the food, Hope turned to leave when I rushed out of the house to catch up with her. "Mommy, can I stay? Please!" I begged mom.

"Yes, you may," she said to my surprise. I was so excited to leave that house again. For just a little while I wouldn't have to worry about hearing Jeffery's footsteps outside my bedroom door. I'd receive a break from the anxiety I suffered, and the smell of Old Spice flooding my room before being violated by a heartless monster. Finally, I would get to sleep in peace.

Hope had a warm, loving, and gentle spirit unlike Jeffery and that creepy old witchdoctor. I felt happy around her, and I even had my own room filled with toys to play with at her house. For a brief moment, I'd become the daughter she always wanted.

I wasn't allowed to attend school after word spread around town that I went to see a "root" doctor. Many parents were afraid to allow their children to interact with me or be anywhere around me. The principal of the school decided to send my school work home with me; this was such a bittersweet moment in my life. I loved being away from Jeffery, but I hated not seeing my brother and friends at school. For me, it seemed as if my life was in a tailspin at such a young age. How could my life be crumbling to pieces when it had barely started? And for what? Jeffery? Because my mom couldn't face the reality of what he was doing to my sister and me at night? I never pictured life being like this. As a child, I believed that bad things only happened to bad people—those who did evil and deserved what they got. So my situation was confusing to me. What did I do to deserve so much pain? What did I do to deserve being alienated, isolated, abused, and robbed of my childhood? Why can't I be happy like the other children?

I stayed with Hope for several weeks. We regularly attended church. I even sang in the choir. My favorite song to lead was "I love you."

> *"I love you.*
> *I love you.*
> *I love you Lord, today...*
> *because you care for me*
> *in such a special way.*
> *That's why my heart is filled with praise."*

I'd sing that song with all of my heart. When I'd finish, people would clap and yell, "Go ahead, baby!" This was a new experience for me, and it felt great. I didn't need to fake being sick, nor did I feel anxious while there. I felt safe and secure. But the day when Hope informed me I had to go home, my heart dropped. Fear and anxiety came rushing back into my body.

"You will not be staying in this house anymore," Hope reiterated. She had a smile on her face, not realizing that I dreaded going back home.

"Why?" I asked her, wondering why I had to leave. She explained to me why, to which I responded, "Why?" Every time she explained to me why I had to go back home, I'd respond with the question "Why?" I forgot about the fact that I still had a mother and siblings to go home to. I didn't want to re-encounter Jeffery. I put Hope under a lot of pressure that day, but she handled it with grace. Of course, my mind was already cooking up a plot to get out of being near Jeffery. There was that tried-and-true tactic of faking sickness; it yielded favorable results in the past.

I only had two more days to spend with Hope; after that, I'd have to return to the living Hell I called home. I wanted to have as much fun as I could with Hope; I wanted to take my mind off of the reality waiting for me at the end of our time together. But still, I couldn't help but think about what would happen once I got home: the molestations, the fighting, the chaos and confusion.

One day, while at Hope's house, I went into the bathroom and knelt and prayed. I asked God not to send me back home. I promised him that I would be a good girl and not get into trouble if I could stay with Hope. After I finished praying, I went back to my bedroom and started playing with my doll baby. At that moment, I felt confident that God would answer my prayer, and I'd get to stay with Hope.

Sunday morning came. Hope cooked us breakfast as usual. She told me once I finished eating to gather my things because I was going home after church. Just the sound of those words made my heart stop. It didn't make sense to me that I had to go back to that place. I just knew God heard my prayer. I suddenly burst into tears. Seeing me sad, Hope promised me that she would always love me and come by to visit me. But that didn't matter much because, at that moment, I felt like everyone I loved had failed me. That day in church, I had a long, sad look on my face. I was inwardly praying for God to do something for me, maybe send a miracle and cause Hope to change her mind about sending me home. Something! But nothing happened. Dread filled my heart when, after church, I found myself in the front seat of her car, heading home to mom and Jeffery.

I was exhausted mentally and emotionally. I couldn't handle being around Jeffery anymore. The next morning after coming home, I told my mom again some of the things Jeffery was doing to me. However, I could never really bring myself to describe in detail the horrible things he did to me. My mind recoiled at the thought of those things. As opposed to acknowledging and showing me pity, compassion, and concern for my wellbeing, mom called my godmother and asked her if I could stay with her for a while. What I wanted was for mom to remove me and my siblings from that man's house. I didn't care if we went back to our first home in the city; anything would have beaten staying at Jeffery's house. Anything! I wanted mom to stop living in denial and accept the truth about our situation—that we were living with an abusive sexual predator. Sadly, she continued to stick her head in the sand and act as if the problem lied with me, not Jeffery; and I couldn't understand why.

NOT JUST ANOTHER PRETTY FACE

Chapter 6
Dad's House

It took too long for someone to hear my cries for help. I'd experienced a five-year hell. I faked being sick to get my mom's attention, experienced ridicule and shame after being sent to a witchdoctor, faced rejection from the people I loved, faced disappointment after disappointment; now, I was going to be free from all of that. I began packing my bags to stay with my grandparents. At first, I was happy to be leaving, but then I thought about who I was leaving behind. My little brother would have to remain in Jeffery's house. He was my heart. He was my best friend, and he meant the world to me. We did everything together—played, cried, laughed, joked, and faced the horrors of that house together. I also thought about the fact that I was leaving my mother, who I loved dearly. She comforted me with the promise of coming back to get me after she found another house.

I lived with my godmother for a few weeks until my dad heard about what had happened to me and came and got me. He was outraged over the news of my ordeal and blamed my mom for everything that happened to me. I overheard him talking to his parents and siblings and telling them that my mother was too unfit to be a parent. They agreed with him; this enraged me. She might have been unfit in many ways, but she was still my mom. It didn't matter what flaws she had. My love for her was unconditional.

It was hard listening to the people bad-mouth my mom. In school, if other children talked about my mom, I would punch them in the face. I couldn't do the same to adults, so I fought back by being rebellious.

My dad went to work daily and worked late into the evenings, so I spent most of my time at my grandparents' house. I didn't like being there because I felt like they treated me differently from the other children; perhaps this was because they didn't like my mom.

Whenever dad would come over, he and his brothers and sisters would get together and play poker for money. One night, while they were together, I could hear them in the kitchen talking, laughing, drinking, and carrying on. While the others were in the kitchen, my uncle called me into the room where he was and asked me to rub his back. I agreed to do so. But while rubbing his back, he turned on his side and began groping my breast and fondling my vagina. A familiar feeling came over me. Jeffery's face flashed before my eyes. I thought I was free, but now I was reliving the nightmare. "Don't tell anyone," he kept repeating. Thankfully, he was interrupted by the sound of my dad's voice calling my name. I hurried up and got out of that room.

"Shenita, gather your belongings so we can go home!"

My dad might have sensed that I was not acting my usual self after I left his parents' house, but he didn't know me enough to know when I was acting differently. He wasn't in my life enough to get to know me. To me, he was almost a stranger. Jeffery abused me at mom's house, and now I was experiencing abuse by the very people he trusted.

I remember sitting in the back seat of his car as he drove home, staring at the sky, looking at the stars. Unwanted thoughts fill my mind. I was taken aback by what had just taken place. The thought of it made my stomach turn, and my skin crawl. This cannot be happening to me again, I thought. I was afraid to tell my dad, thinking he wouldn't believe me. After all, everyone liked my uncle.

When I got home, I went straight to my room and laid down. "What makes me different? Why do people that I love hurt me?" I asked myself while lying in bed. I wanted my mom, and I missed my little brother. I began wondering about his safety. That night, I cried myself asleep.

The next morning, an unfamiliar face greeted me; her name was Tiffany; she was my dad's new girlfriend. Dad said she was going to be like my mom. But I didn't like her. And truthfully, it wasn't her that was the issue.

I couldn't accept the idea of some other woman taking the place of my mom. I made up my mind. I wasn't going to listen to her, my dad, or anyone who wasn't my mom. I was going to show both of them that this woman was not my mom, and I did just that.

Good News

While I was getting dressed for school, the telephone rang. It was my mom; she was calling for my dad. I stopped getting dressed and began eavesdropping on their conversation. I could hear her asking him for his help. She wanted him to let my little brother come and live with us, at least until she found a stable home. She said that she discovered that what my brother and I had been telling her for years was the truth: her boyfriend, Jeffery, had molested me and was in an open relationship with her oldest daughter. Amazingly, Jeffery and Shasha told her to pack her things and leave *their* house. Dad was speechless. Shock was all over his face. I waited for the two of them to finish talking so I could speak to her. I ran to him and asked, "Can I talk to my mommy?" He then handed me the telephone. "Hi, mommy. When are you coming to get me?" She paused and avoided my question, changing the subject instead.

"I love you. I will talk to you later, okay? Bye." Before I could say *I love you*, I heard the phone click, and then I heard a buzzing noise.

"Hello! Hello!"

"Hang the phone up. Your mother hung up on you," dad said harshly. I hung up the telephone feeling heartbroken, then turned away to continue getting dressed for school. I then heard someone yell,

"Hurry up!" It was my dad's girlfriend. When she said that, I looked at her and rolled my eyes. *How dare she talk to me in that tone?* I thought. *Who does she think she is?*

"I don't like you! You are not my momma! You can't tell me what to do!" I said.

"I don't like you either with your sassy behind! You better be quiet before I tell your dad."

"I do not care! Tell him!" I stomped my feet while walking away. I then slammed the door behind me. "I hate my dad. I hate his stupid girlfriend. I hate Jeffery. I hate everyone who hurt me and talked bad about my mom," I muttered to myself. That morning, I went to school with an attitude; I was angry. However, my day got better when I saw my little brother in the hallway. I ran over to him and gave him the biggest, tightest hug. "Guess what? You are coming to stay with dad!" I told him. He smiled and then walked away.

Seeing Roger again caused my heart to overflow with joy and excitement. While in class, I was daydreaming about all of the things we were going to do together once he got to dad's house. Three o'clock came quickly. The bell rang! I ran as fast as I could to make sure my brother got on the bus with me. I felt like I was his protector. When we got on the bus, I asked him all kinds of questions. I even asked if Jeffrey touched his private parts. "No!" he replied, looking at me like I was crazy. He did tell me about how Shasha made him walk for two miles all alone in the hot sun to the store to buy her some sweets, and how she beat him for spending her change—she sent him outside to pick switches, dipped them in water, and then whipped him with them. He showed me the welts the beating left on his body. I already disliked Shasha for the way she treated my mom, and I despised her even more for her relationship with Jeffery, now I hated her for what she did to Roger. *How could she hurt someone as sweet and innocent as him?* I thought.

"Where was mommy? Did you tell her?"

"Mommy was not home; and no, I didn't tell her. I was too afraid of getting a beating again when she was not at home." When he told me that, my heart got heavy. I endured abuse at the hands of Jeffery, but our sister was abusing him, and I wasn't there to protect him. *Maybe I should have kept quiet and allowed Jeffery to continue to hurt me. At least, I would have been ther for Roger*, I thought. I promised him I would never leave him again, no matter what. I couldn't stand to hear about the abuses he endured any longer, so I quickly changed the subject.

The school bus arrived at my grandparents' house. As soon as my grandmother saw Roger get off the bus, she yelled at him and said, "Get right back on that bus! What are you coming here for? No one told me anything about watching you!" Grandma didn't care too much for Roger, mainly because she didn't believe he was my dad's biological son. She had openly complained before about his dark skin tone and claimed that he was the son of a man my mom dated before my dad, even though a DNA test showed he was 99% my dad's biological son.

CHAPTER 6: DAD'S HOUSE

Roger didn't say a word. I could see the disappointment in his eyes as he turned and walked away. But I wasn't worried about his safety because I knew he was going to my uncle's house down the road. Still, hearing my grandmother talk to him that way deeply disturbed me. I could only wonder about how he was feeling after that experience.

Once Roger was out of view, I ran into grandma's house and jumped into the bed with tears streaming down my face. I began to pray, "God, please help my mom find a house. Everywhere we go, people are mean to us, and some of them do and say bad things to us. I don't like being here, nor at my dad's house. I want my mommy! God, please! My brother and I need your help, in Jesus' name, amen."

When my dad came to pick me up, he asked, "Where is Yaya (Roger's nickname)?" I told him where he was and what grandma said to him. He didn't bother confronting her over her hurtful words; it wasn't a shock to him because he already knew how she felt. He respected her feelings and asked my uncle to watch him while he worked. That was another way they kept my brother and me apart. That was a tough time in my life. Everyone I loved hurt me in some way or another except for my brother. He was all I had and the reason I didn't lose my sanity.

Rebellious

Although I was no longer at Jeffery's house, I wasn't out of the danger zone. I still had predators around me. Being at my grandparents' house was simply a change of scenery, but it contained many of the same abusive elements I experienced at the place I came from. I still felt compelled to sleep with one eye open at night, afraid that someone would try to take advantage of me to fulfill their perverse cravings. It seemed like this nightmare was never going to end, and like morning would never come, but it did. The next morning, I picked myself up and got prepared for school. I never adapted to living with my dad and his parents. I was still anticipating my mother coming to get me and take me home with her. I even felt irked that my dad took me away from her. Out of anger towards my situation, I started acting out in class. I started jumping on the desks, turning over the chairs and yelling loud and uncontrollably. The teacher threatened to call my dad because she couldn't get a handle on me. She ended up sending me to the principal's office, and I got expelled for ten days.

I knew my dad was going to tear my butt up when I got home, but I didn't care. I was full of pain that had turned into rage over being separated from my mom. I wanted him to understand my pain.

My daily routine was exhausting. I'd get up, go to school with an attitude, get off the bus, go straight to my bedroom, jump in the bed, and cry myself to sleep. My sleep was usually interrupted by nightmares of Jeffery—seeing his horrible face, smelling his Old Spice cologne, feeling his nasty fingers on my skin and his hot breath in my ears. I'd wake up sweating profusely with my heart beating fast, and would struggle to attempt to go back to sleep. This pattern continued for a very long time. My grandmother even tried to convince my dad that I was pregnant because of my sleep patterns. She urged him to take me to the doctor immediately. He agreed.

Unfortunately, my dad wasn't very encouraging or supportive of me during this time. He'd say things to me to belittle me and make me feel low; it was as if he secretly despised me. For what? I don't know. I'd try to share my heart with him, but he didn't want to hear my side of the story. It seemed as if no one wanted to hear what I had to say. They were all too busy making decisions for me and talking about me to talk to me and ask me what I wanted. I explained to my dad that I was not having intercourse, but he didn't listen. After grandma suggested to him I might be pregnant, dad asked his girlfriend, Tiffany, to take me to the Health Department to have a pregnancy test done the following day. I was twelve-years-old.

Due to my age, I had to undergo a full examination while at the clinic. The doctor introduced himself to me and asked me to get undressed. He explained step-by-step what he was going to do. I was okay until he asked me to spread my legs apart so that he could insert a small instrument and his fingers into my vagina. I was nervous; hesitant. I tensed up. The doctor continuously asked me to keep my legs spread while he performed the examination. Even though Tiffany was in the room with me, I was afraid. I was very uncomfortable because all I could picture was Jeffery's face between my legs.

The pregnancy test came back negative, but the

examination revealed that I'd had intercourse before. I thought for sure this would not only convince my dad that what he'd learned about my past with Jeffery was true, but that it would cause him to become more sympathetic towards me, but it didn't. Rather than showing compassion for his little girl who was a victim of rape and molestation, he came down on me hard, stating that he'd no longer allow me to attend after-school activities. "You are a liar! Fast and grown!" he yelled at me. I was in tears, feeling torn to pieces. *How could he say those things to me? He didn't ask me any questions; he just jumped straight to accusations. He didn't give me the chance to plead my case. But I was the victim! I did nothing wrong; I was the one who was wronged! And yet, I was being treated like I was a criminal.*

Looking back in hindsight, I've often wondered if guilt was eating him alive. Was he masking his sense of failure as a father, feeling bad because he wasn't there to protect me? Just something to think about. Sometimes, I wondered if the truth was better left unsaid. In either case, I began hating my dad after that day.

When I returned home, I packed my clothes and secretly shared with my brother that I was going to run away and look for mom. I didn't care about the consequences. I realized that had dad caught me, he'd discipline me pretty hard just like the other times I got in trouble, but I didn't care. I wanted my mom, but it was my brother who changed my mind. He begged me not to leave. The only thing that stopped me from running away that day is my little brother—I didn't want to leave him behind. But that was just *that* day.

"I'm Running Away!"

Mom finally found a place to live. When she came to pick us up, she had the brightest smile on her face. She was proud that she had fulfilled her promise to us. However, her happiness and joy vanished after my dad told her she could not take me with her. The two of them bickered back and forth, blaming each other for the things done to me. "You just want to keep them so you will not have to pay child support!" mom shouted.

"You don't want them! You just want my check and food stamps!" dad fired back. Neither of them thought about the fact that their words would have lasting effects on their children's self-esteem. They didn't care that we were present and listening.

Were they speaking the truth? Did they want us only for their financial gain? Now, I was beginning to question both of them, wondering if either of them truly loved my brother and me. I felt like it was Roger and me against the world. Eventually, mom and dad reached an agreement: Roger would stay with mom, and I would stay with dad. *This has to be some sort of sick joke,* I thought. Neither of them cracked a smile. I couldn't understand why my mom gave me up so easily. She promised me that she would take me with her once she found someplace to live. And how could my dad be so cruel as not to allow me to go with her? It's not like he genuinely wanted me, I felt. He shattered my hopes and dreams in that very moment.

As my mom and brother turned and walked away, I looked my dad in his eyes and told him I hated him and that there was nothing he could do to keep me away from my mom. He warned me to be quiet, but I didn't heed the warning. I kept expressing to him my feelings. Eventually, the altercation went from an argument to a fistfight. Perhaps I wasn't in my right mind at the time. I knew better. I learned to "honor thy mother and thy father and thy days on earth shall be longer," but all of that went out of the window. All Hell had broken loose! "Every time you leave, I am going to run away! Hit me again! I don't care! There's nothing you can do to hurt me anymore! I hate you, and you are a sorry excuse for a man! You never did anything for me anyway!" My voice was trembling as I shouted, and tears were pouring from my eyes down my cheeks.

"Shut up, right now! You just want to go with your mom so you can be a whore and do what you want to do!" After my dad said that, I was so furious, I started biting my lips until they bled. My dad took me to my grandfather's house and explained to him what was going on. He said he "washed his hands with me," and that there was nothing left for him to do but send me away.

"You listen, and you listen to me good! Do not ever give up on her. You continue to talk to her no matter what. Pray and hope that one day, before it's too late, she will listen."

My dad had to go to the store to pick up some items. He demanded that I not leave the house for anything. As soon as I saw him pull off and his car was no longer in sight, I called my aunt and asked her to come and get me. I was crying. She agreed. When my dad returned home, I wasn't there. He went out and searched for me. After several hours, he spotted me walking down the road. He immediately jumped out of the car, and the chase began. I was running like a deer through the forest frightened by the sounds of gunshots. I ran inside of a neighbor's house; I was shaken and crying. I begged her not to open the door for my dad because I was afraid for my life. That neighbor finally called the police, and her brother, who was an officer, showed up.

The officer restrained me and placed me inside his car. Unfortunately, I had to return home with my dad. I cursed both he and my dad out. Before I knew it, my dad's hand was going across the left side of my face. "I'm calling social service! I am going to show them my bruises and tell them you abused me!" I yelled. I reached for the phone, but he snatched it away from me. Then with a hurt voice, he said,

"If you want your mother that bad, I will take you to her. Don't call me when you are hungry! Or when you have no place to stay! Or when you end up pregnant! I am done with you!"

Little did I know, I was embarking up several trials and tribulations that would last nearly two decades.

My dad watched me while I packed my belongings. He wanted to make sure I did not leave anything. The drive to my mom's new house was interesting. Where she lived, it was so quiet, you could hear a pin drop. As I exited the car, I was expecting him to say "I love you";

instead, he simply sped off without saying a word, leaving skid marks in the road. In retrospect, my dad only wanted the best for me and did what he thought was the best thing for me at the time.

My mom and brother were standing on the porch, waiting for me. They were happy to see me. We reminisced over all of the things we'd gone through together. We joked and laughed about it. We were immature to think such things were funny. It didn't take long for familiar habits to return. My mom was hardly ever home again. My oldest sister and her newborn daughter moved in with us. She resumed her position of providing for me and Roger and keeping us safe. But nurturing a newborn while trying to look after me and my brother became overwhelming to her. She eventually decided to move into her own place with her child. I wanted to go with them. I begged her to take me and Roger with her, but she kindly reminded me that she was not our mother and explained that she had to do what was best for her. Still, I was content being with my mom and brother again, just the three of us. However, this didn't erase the empty feeling I had inside. I felt neglected and unloved while there because we didn't spend quality time together. We may have had food, we may have had a place to lay our heads, we may have had most of the basic necessities to live, but the one thing we didn't have much of was the most important thing: love. Without that, nothing else mattered much. I knew mom loved me, but I wanted her to show it.

Chapter 7
Welcome To The Team

It was springtime, and it was my seventh grade school year. The flowers were blooming, pollen falling, and the smell of newness was in the air. I was the envy of many teenagers: I was smart; had long, thick hair; and a figure-eight frame with pretty legs and a flat stomach. I was beautiful. For the first time in a long time, I was able to live a "normal" life. However, I still struggled to block out the pain of my past from my mind.

One day during Physical Education (PE), a group of us teenagers got together and began talking about how fun sex was to them. Immediately, I thought about Jeffery again, and also that day at the clinic when the doctor examined me. How could they think sex was fun? The thought of it made me sick. My friend Shalya asked me if I'd ever had sex, and I replied, "No!"

"Well, you do not know what you are missing," she responded. I just laughed.

"Girl, you are crazy!" After that, my friends began to tease me, calling me a virgin. If only they knew my past, I thought.

Later that evening, a boy from PE class showed up at my doorstep. I stood at the door in amazement. "Well, are you going to let me in, or are you going to just stand there?" he asked.

"I'm sorry. Come in. My mind was somewhere else." I was flattered that he even noticed me, and I was honored that he was standing in my living room. He was dark-complexioned, and he had a well-trimmed mustache and sideburns. He was handsome. All the girls adored him. He had a New York City accent, wore stylish clothes, and knew how to charm the ladies to get what he wanted. Rumor around the school was that he was a "player".

He whispered sweet things in my ears: "You are the prettiest girl in school. I want you to be my girl. I promise if you have sex with me, it will not hurt. I will not tell anyone." Those words made my heart melt, and he led me into my bedroom with my pants half down. As he pulled down his pants, I began to wonder to myself, What am I doing? I wanted to tell him to stop, but for whatever reason, I felt speechless and paralyzed. He proceeded to do his thing while I just laid there, picturing Jeffery's face.

Suddenly, I felt something warm run down my leg. I touched my leg to see what it was, and I discovered that my menstrual cycle came on. I forcefully pushed him off of me, which upset him. "I am not finished yet!"

he yelled, but I ignored him and rushed in the bathroom. While there, I laid on the floor in the fetal position and rocked back and forth, wondering what I had done.

Different scenes from my past began to play in my head. I felt dizzy, lightheaded like I'd just gotten off of a merry-go-round. I just wanted my mother. I needed her. I needed to feel her arms around me, and I needed to hear her voice say, "It is okay, baby. Mommy is here." But she wasn't there. When I finally came back to, I wiped the tears from my eyes, cleaned myself up, and wiped the blood off of the floor, and regrouped. Just then, I heard my dad's voice saying,

"See, I told you. You are going to end up pregnant." For a brief moment, I began to believe I was everything he claimed I was: a whore, fast, good for nothing. While thinking these thoughts, I went back to my bedroom to clean up the mess I had made. I was afraid my mom was going to find my bloody sheets. So I put the sheets in a bag and threw them into a neighbor's trash can, then I went back inside, got in my bed, and cried myself to sleep. I hoped the nights of crying myself to sleep were over, but they weren't. Crying myself to sleep had become a routine of mine.

The next day in school, people were looking at me strangely; they were whispering to each other laughing when I passed by. I did not know what was going on; and then my friend Shayla came to me and said, "Have you heard? You are the talk of the school."

"No. Why do you say that? And why am I the talk of the school?"

"You made out with Tony last night at your house. He told everyone he had to stop because you were on your period." My heart skipped a beat. He lied to me. He promised me he would not tell anyone, and now the entire school knew I slept with him; and to make matters worse, he told them I was on my period! I started to cry. Shayla took my hand and led me into the girl's restroom, wiped my face and told me not to worry. She said he did every girl he made out with the same way, so relax and "welcome to the team." That phrase ("welcome to the team") played over and over again in my head.

I felt like I was being passed around like a football. I never spoke to that boy after that. How could he deceive me like that? How could I be so naive as to think he would not tell anyone about us. I went home and prayed, "God, please give me my own baby, a child that will love me no matter what. I promise, God if you do, I will be the best mom ever. I promise I will never leave it. Please, God, I just want someone to love me back. In Jesus name, amen!" A thirteen-year-old child shouldn't be praying to be a mother so that she can feel loved; she should be praying that she makes the cheerleader squad or the basketball team. But I had reached a place of desperation, and felt like this was the only way to find someone who would love me. That's how large the void in my soul was. I didn't know about the love of God, and my quest for man's love would take me down an even darker road. And it all began with an older boy I met.

Chapter 8

Monster

My mom's house was the hangout out spot. All of the older guys (nineteen-years-old and older) came to see my sister and my older brother, who lived down the street. One day, we were all sitting on the porch, laughing and joking, when my cousin came over with his friend, Fred. I instantly gravitated to him. He had a distinct swag about himself. He was muscular and talked very proper. He wore bifocals and had an attitude. He spoke about how he liked to fight and how people feared him. That should have been my cue that he was dangerous, but my immaturity and desperation sent me right into the arms of a maniac.

There was something different about him at the beginning, which is what drew me to him. To this day, I can't say what it was, but he certainly appealed to me. Maybe it was my desperation to be loved or his aggressive nature that lured me—that aggression made him seem like a protector. But we began to talk. Fred would come over to my house every afternoon. We'd laugh, joke, play, and share our deepest secrets. He'd listen while I poured out my feelings to him, revealing to him everything I endured. My sister noticed how close me and Fred were becoming, and she politely reminded him of my age. She reminded him that he was too old for me and that she disapproved of the two of us being together. "C'mon, now! I look at her as my little sister!" Fred replied. He convinced my sister that there was nothing sexual between him and me, and he promised her he would never betray her trust. Later that day, we met up again. I asked him if he would have sex with me so I could have his baby. With no hesitation, he agreed.

Now, that was not Fred's original plan, but he was more than willing to go along with it. We made plans to meet the next day at his friend's house. He explained to me that I had to keep everything we did a secret or he could go to jail if anyone found out about us. I was very excited! The man that I had bonded with agreed to impregnate me! I rushed home to come up with a master plan to meet with him the next day.

While my parents were doing their thing, their thirteen-year-old daughter was making plans to have a baby with an adult male she barely knew, a plan that would affect her for the rest of her life. The next day, I skipped school and met Fred at the designated location. When I arrived at his friend's house, I could not help but notice that she was upset and felt uneasy about me being there. I later found out that she had slept with him the day before, and she was carrying his child. We proceeded with our plan. That day (July 28, 1993) was one of the happiest days of my life. A feeling came over me, and I knew deep down inside that I'd accomplished my mission; I knew a baby was making its way into my womb.

The next afternoon, I waited on my porch for Fred like before, but he didn't show up. I was worried, thinking something was wrong. I went to where he usually hung out, but no one had seen him or heard from him all day. Later that evening, I saw my cousin who shared with me some devastating news: Fred went back to New York to live. "Stop playing!" I said.

"No, I am not playing. He didn't tell you that he was only down for a couple months?" I could not believe what I was hearing. My mind began to race. "He tricked me! He lied to me just so he could have sex with me! Why didn't he tell me he was leaving? Why didn't he ask me to go?" I said. I then turned and walked away crying, feeling crushed and useless.

My First Pregnancy

I prayed that Fred would call me. I needed to tell him that my menstrual cycle was late and that I was vomiting every morning. I couldn't tell my mom. I knew she would be upset and send him to jail. I kept it a secret as long as I could. The stomach cramps, the headaches, feeling of fatigue, and vomiting was too much for a child to bear alone, so I finally told my sister what I had done. She took me to the Health Department to confirm whether or not I was pregnant. While we were waiting for the test results, she drilled me about who the father was. I was afraid to tell her, knowing she would be disappointed. The nurse called us into her office and revealed that the results were positive.

My sister and I cried, but mine were tears of joy. She then promised me that she would let me tell mom on my own, but reneged on her promise once we got home. "Ma! Ma! Ma! Tina has something to tell you!" she blabbed.

"No, I don't, Ma," I said.

"Okay, Ma, Tina is pregnant!" Before I could say a word, I found myself ducking a Champagne bottle that was flying my way; it was only inches away from hitting my head.

"You will never see daylight again! You will not have that baby! Get out of my face!" mom yelled.

"Yes, I am! I am going to have my baby, or I will run away!" I screaming those words, I ran out of the house crying and wondering if mom was going to make me abort the baby.

When I returned home, mom had calmed down. "Who is the baby's father?" she asked.

"It's Fred's baby." After relaying that information, I begged her not to press charges against him. She called his mom and informed her of the news. His mom immediately called him, but he denied having any sexual contact with me. My mom assured him that if he did not own up to his responsibility, he would regret it. After drilling him, he told the truth and asked her for forgiveness. He promised to come back to North Carolina to take care of his child. Not long after that, he returned, and I began to see Fred's true colors.

The Real Fred

Before my pregnancy, Fred was a loving, caring, gentle and compassionate person, a shoulder I could cry on, but after the pregnancy, he became someone I didn't recognize. He once wiped my tears away, and now he had become the source of my tears. It started subtly but escalated quickly. First, there were the harsh insults, the rude comments, and the mean stares. After that, I began to experience the terror that so many battered women experienced. A little push turned into a hard shove, and then from there, it was a hard slap to the face. Eventually, that open hand became a balled fist and Fred began punching me like I was his punching bag.

As the days went by, Fred grew bolder and bolder with his assaults. I can remember the two of us sitting on the bed one day; I was in a good mood, especially since we were only four weeks away from the delivery time. Fred was talking to me about something; I was reading some literature on what to expect in the final trimester. I was listening to him, but I did not look him in the eyes while he was talking; this set him off, causing him to lose control suddenly. He then jumped up and attempted to kick me in my face. I moved out of the way to avoid taking the shot to the face, but his kick ended up landing on my stomach. It was so painful and terrifying. I began to yell loudly. Just then, he wrapped his arms around my neck and squeezed so tightly I couldn't breathe. I tried with all my might to remove his arms so I could get some air, but I was helpless and unable to break free. Gradually, my vision faded to black as I passed out.

When I finally awoke, I was on the floor, blowing bubbles out of my mouth. Fred was looming over my body, calling my name. When my mom entered into the room and saw me on the floor, she started screaming. "What happened to my baby?!" I was in a state of shock, discombobulated, and unable to speak. My mom rushed me to the hospital. When I arrived, the nurses had to stop me from going into pre-term labor. After I was stable, a nurse requested to speak to me privately. She wanted to know what really caused me to go into early labor. She was very wise and didn't fall for my lie, claiming I fell. She could see the fear in my eyes and suspected that Fred had something to do with it. Part of me wanted to tell her what Fred had done to me, but then I worried that if I told her she would alert the authorities and Fred would end up going to jail; then he wouldn't be able to be a part of me and the baby's lives. I didn't want that, so I didn't tell the nurse the truth of what happened. I buried the truth in my heart and told myself that Fred might not have done what he did if I didn't make him feel disrespected. I blamed myself for his actions. Of course, Fred promised not to hurt me again after that, and I believed him, but that promise didn't hold out for long. There were plenty more beatings to come. There would be several more times my neck would end up in his arms, and I'd get choked until I nearly died, all because I either didn't do something he told me to do or I made him feel disrespected in some way.

I was plummeting into a deep pit of terror, one that was even worse than Jeffery. Fred's behavior was getting more and more out of control until the point of total obsession. He not only controlled me with violence but began to threaten my life. He made it clear to me that if he could not have me, then no one could. I didn't know what to say or what to do behind all of this. The only thing I knew to do was pretend like nothing was happening to me. So I'd pile on the makeup to hide the bruises, and come up with elaborate excuses to explain away the bruises around my neck whenever asked about them. Still, I was terrified of him; and yet, I felt sorry for him at the same time. I felt sorry that he and his mother didn't have the best relationship, and that he felt as if she didn't love him. I began to convince myself that I could change him and help him heal by loving him more and doing everything he asked me to. For this to work, I had to be careful of everything I said and did around him. It was like walking on eggshells around him—don't speak too fast; don't say the wrong thing; don't tick him off in any way. The penalty for breaking his rules (even the ones he never communicated) was another beating. And he didn't care that I was carrying his child. My body would tense up around him. Whenever he'd try to kiss or hug me, I'd immediately jerk away out of fear, thinking he was trying to attack me. I so wanted to tell my mom and dad what Fred was doing to me so that they could rescue me, but I was too afraid to do so. So I simply cried within and prayed for God to protect the baby and me.

Chapter 9
New Beginnings

On April 15, 1994, at 6:30 am, my water broke. I was anticipating the birth of my son, who would be the love of my life. Me, my mom, and Fred rushed to the hospital. When we arrived, they admitted immediately. My doctor was Dr. Smith. She examined me. I appreciate her professionalism in pretending she didn't see anything wrong with a thirteen-year-old girl delivering a baby. She treated me like any other patient. But I'm sure she expressed her hidden concerns and disappointment to her colleagues.

While lying in that hospital room, the contractions started coming in. As the pain intensified, so did my anxiety. I didn't know what was happening to me. I had never encountered such excruciating pain before. I felt a strong urge to push with each contraction. The midwife warned me that pushing before the full dilation of ten centimeters was dangerous for both the baby and me, but I desperately wanted to get him out of me. "I can't help it! I have to pushhhhhhhh!!! Please pull him out!!!" I begged.

I was so drained. My dad came in to visit me. He saw me in agony and pain, trying to push the baby out. "Are you okay?" he asked upon seeing me grimacing in pain.

"No! I am in so much pain!"

"Good enough for you," he said before turning and abruptly exiting the room, leaving me to suffer alone.

At 11:32 pm, just twenty-eight minutes before my fourteenth birthday, I pushed a 7 lbs, 14 oz baby boy out of me at only eight centimeter. Due to not following the midwife's instruction to not push before dilating to 10 cm, I tore my vagina from front to back during the process of giving birth to my son. I had to receive eighty stitches inside and outside of my vagina. But the pain was worth it. The moment I looked into my son's eyes, I fell in love with him and forgot about everything else. I held him close to my chest. I wanted his name to have a meaning, so I named him Emmanuel (which means "God is with us") Malik (which means "King of Kings") James. God answered my prayer. I finally had someone that would love me no matter the circumstances.

After a few days in the hospital, they discharged me with a special instruction that read, "Patient is to sit on a soft pillow for two weeks following a saline and saltwater cleaning after each visit to the bathroom. The Patient is to follow up with her gynecologist to check proper healing of the vaginal area." I believed my life was complete now that I had a son, and that the violence Fred inflicted on me would finally come to an end. After all, I'd just given him his first son. Sadly, the violence didn't end. It got worse. Far worse.

Fed Up

The beatings came more frequently. Slaps, kicks, punches to the face, getting choked; Fred was a monster. I began to feel like I was now his slave. He'd do these things in front of our baby. Things got so bad I felt like I'd reached my breaking point. I didn't know how much more of this I could take. I began contemplating running away from Fred, but again, I was afraid of the unknown; furthermore, I was afraid of what Fred might do to me had he caught me trying to escape. But I knew I had to do something. Things couldn't continue on the way they were. Either I was going to run or stand up and fight. Perhaps that's what it all came down to. It was either him or me. And the more I thought about my son, the greater the sense of urgency overtook me. Something has to change now!

While Fred was sitting in the bedroom, feeding the baby, I was reflecting over my life. I was tired of lying for him and covering up the bruises. I'd concluded that I was no longer going to endure physical, mental, and emotional abuse. At this point, I preferred to die rather than continue to live with Fred. So I mustered up the courage to confront him and inform him that our relationship was over. I anticipated the worse—a punch to the face, barrage of strikes and blows, being strangled until unconscious or dead—but was pleasantly surprised when he calmly responded, "Okay." He then continued to feed the baby.

In the upcoming months, I did my best to avoid Fred. We didn't have sex, and I refused to be left alone with him. I'd been traumatized by him and didn't want anything more to do with him. But I knew he was unpredictable and capable of anything. I witnessed him beat a man with a baseball bat for leaving him in New York City. From that day on, I didn't trust Fred. Sure, he may say one thing, but his volatile nature wouldn't allow him to let me go and walk away. He wanted full control of everyone and everything. And this was evidenced by the fact that, although I expressed to him that I was through with him, he still took it upon himself to try to control where I went and who I talked to.

One Friday night, my sister agreed to watch my baby and give me some free time. I went to a basketball game at a recreational center with a male friend. I was sitting on the top bleachers watching the player shoot three-pointers and dunk the ball when I looked up and saw Fred standing in front of me. His eyes were bloodshot red, and he had a perplexed expression on his face. I sensed something awful was about to take place. He asked me to go outside so that he could speak with me alone. He claimed that what he had to say would only take a minute. But before I could say anything, he grabbed my feet, dragged me from the top bleacher, and started punching me in my face while calling me names.

"Bitch, I told you if I can't have you, no one can!" The referee stopped the game, ran over and pulled him off of me.

Frightened and embarrassed, I laid on the cold, dirty floor, balled up in the fetal position, crying and wondering, *Why me?* By then, the police arrived and issued a warrant for Fred's arrest. Now, I could no longer hide my abuse. A crowd of people had just witnessed one of the brutal beatings I endured day after day. An ambulance arrived, and EMTs took pictures of my bruises and bloody clothes. They then took me to Vermont Hospital. The State decided to press charges against him. Even then, I wanted to protect him, and even asked the nurse not to press charges against him. She looked at me confused, and then responded, "Ma'am, it is our policy." At that point, I realized there was nothing I could do. I started to feel sorry for Fred as if I'd done something wrong. I mean, he was the father of my child. I didn't want my son to grow up without a father. However, part of me spoke up and reminded me that this was not the type of life I was meant to live. God didn't design me to be someone's punching bag, and my son didn't need to grow up in a war-zone, watching mommy get beaten and abused in every way possible. I needed to emancipate myself from the abuse, once and for all, and rediscover what it means to be alive.

What looked like a bad situation turned out for my good. That Friday sparked the beginning of new freedom for me. During the trial, I had to testify against Fred. I recounted the events that took place that Friday, and also about the nature of our relationship—all of the abusive things Fred did to me. I laid it all out, testifying against him. I was nervous, but as I continued, I felt empowered as if I was wrenching my life out of his hands and taking it back. The more I spoke up rather than trying to cover up for Fred, the more liberated I felt, and the more confident I became. I needed that. I needed to hear myself recount the events of our time together. I needed to hear myself describe the beatings, the strangulations, and the threats Fred dealt me. Hearing the details, even from my mouth, painted a grim picture of what it was like living with a monster.

After the court hearing, Fred and I went our separate ways. He attempted to maintain contact with our son, but drugs and violence ripped him out of our lives. The rest of Fred's life was marred by addictions and bouts of violence that landed him in and out of prison. Sadly, he'd go on to find other women, and do to them what he'd done to me.

Chapter 10
Tricked Into Tricking

Now that Fred was entirely out of my life, I felt free; however, the reality that I was now a single parent, a teenage mother, set in. How am I going to eat? Who's going to supply for the baby? Who'll take care of us? I had plenty of concerns but no solutions. So I decided to go back to school. I realized I was not like the other young girls—I didn't think like them, I didn't talk like them, and I didn't look like them. I was ashamed of my body. The flat stomach I once had was now a flabby mess covered with dark red stretch marks, my breasts were much larger than the other girls because of the milk inside of them, and my hips had expanded two sizes.

I remember walking down the ninth grade hallway, holding my breath and holding my stomach in. I was met with critical, condescending expressions by my peers. I could hear some of them whispering, "She had a baby." But I just held my head up and smiled, trying my best to remain strong amidst the giggles and whispers. I was sleep-deprived because of the baby and burdened down with adult cares and pressures. My peers hadn't had a clue what it was like being in my shoes. I was tired, and now, I felt I wasn't ready for this type of pressure. So when no one was looking, I took the first exit door I saw and never returned to Dodge High School.

I was disappointed in myself. I was lost, ashamed, and confused. I wasn't old enough to work. I was a high school drop-out. I had a baby. I had no financial support and no stable place to call home. God! What is next?!

Fast Money

It was a hot summer day in June of 1995, and I was walking to clear my mind. I needed to figure out how to provide for my baby and me. At first, I was not paying attention to my surroundings. However, I happened to notice out the corner of my eye a middle-aged man approaching me while riding a candy apple red beach cruiser bike. Before I knew it, he was right beside me. He was dressed flamboyantly and sported a flashy gold chain. My first thought was he was a pimp or a drug dealer. He was not physically attractive; he was short and stocky with a belly protruding from his pants. He smiled, revealing a gold tooth. He lustfully stared at me. "Hello, beautiful," he said in a provocative tone. "What's your name? And why is a pretty lady walking alone?"

"My name is Tina, and I'm walking alone to clear my mind."

CHAPTER 10: TRICKED INTO TRICKING

"How would you like to make some easy money?" I was still walking and pretending to no hear him. At the same time, I was trying to figure him out. What kind of easy money was he talking about?

"You can make some easy money with that body of yours."

My body? I thought to myself; this is the same body I was ashamed of. But he gave me his pager number and told me to think about it, and then he rode off.

At the time, I was wearing a pair of white daisy dukes and a fitted orange spaghetti strap top with a plunging neckline. I wasn't trying to be seductive, but evidently, he saw something that made him approach me. Hmm, I thought, this could this be the answer to my problems. Could I really make enough money to take care of my baby and me? I began to convince myself that I needed to use my body to make money. What other choice did I have? Starve? Let my baby starve? Oh no! I am going to see what this man has to offer.

I began to get excited over the prospect of making money. I rushed over to my sister's house and eagerly paged the man and then waited for him to call. Within five minutes, he called, and uttered confidently, "I knew you would call." We made arrangements to meet at a motel. I wasn't comfortable with meeting in a motel, considering that the ones I'd seen were generally run down with disgusting-looking rooms. But I agreed to go through with it. I went to a motel. When I entered the room, the man was stretched out on the bed wearing only a pair of navy blue boxers. There was the sight of that disgusting pop-belly again, looking like he was nine months pregnant. *Yuck! I can't do this*, I thought. He looked like an old, nasty man laying on that bed. And the room itself was a turnoff. Ripped wallpaper hung on the walls, there were several stains on the floor, and condom wrappers were everywhere. The smell of cheap cologne, sweat, and intercourse filled the room.

While lying there, the man had the biggest smile on his face, looking at me like I was prey. I began to wonder if the money was even worth it. *Is this what he thinks of me? Did I look that desperate and needy when he first saw me?* I was just ready to get everything over with. He pulled out a fresh condom and threw the wrapper on the floor, adding to the collection of other wrappers on the floor. He then proceeded to have intercourse with me. While he was on top of me, I was thinking, *What am I doing? This can't be happening!* Approximately two minutes later, he withdrew from me and handed me a large wad of cash. The moment I looked at the wad of cash, all those other thoughts went away. I placed the money in my bra and quickly exited the room. "I just made $200 in two minutes!" I said to myself. I had never seen that much money before. *This is way too much money for a fifteen-year-old girl*, I thought.

I began seeing that man regularly. As he said, it was easy money. However, lodged in the back of my mind during each meet-up was the question, *Shenita, what are you doing?* Every time I questioned my actions, I came up with an excuse to justify what I was doing. I even told myself I was doing the right thing for my baby. And yet, each sexual encounter brought back painful memories from my past. I would see Jeffery's face every time. After the man was done having intercourse with me and then handed me some money, I thought about the time Jeffery was finished with me and then gave me a ten-dollar bill. It was that same cheap, used feeling that came over me. But I continued to do what I was doing, hoping to save up enough money to change my circumstances.

I thought I'd saved up enough money to rent out the house next door to my sister's house. I'd be able to move me, my son, and Roger into it. It was a small, two-bedroom white house with green sidings. The yard was full of pine trees and pine cones. One morning, I saw the owner of the house working in the yard. He was a very dark complexion man with pearly white teeth and a clean haircut. I decided to inquire about renting the house. He invited me inside of the property and gave me a tour of the house. While there, I told to him that I wanted to rent it, but I only saved up enough money for the first month's rent. I asked him if he would work with me on the deposit. Why did I say that? At that moment, an expression came over his face, and I knew where things were headed; I could see it in his eyes. Before that, he was speaking very articulately and intelligently and acting very professional, but after I asked him to work something out with me, his whole demeanor and tone of voice changed. Now, lust was in his eyes. From that look, I knew what he wanted. Reluctantly, I agreed to have sex with him as a down-payment on the property. He led me down a narrow hallway and laid me on the floor, then he pulled my pants down, put on a red condom, and began having intercourse with me. I just laid there, staring off into the distance with tears streaming down my face.

While he was on top of me, I started praying silently, "God, why is this happening to me? Please save me from having to do this." I began reliving the past. I felt filthy and disgusting. I began begging the man, "Hurry up, please! Just hurry up!" He gained a sense of pleasure from hearing me beg and cry during the ordeal; this made him moan and gyrate even harder. Those five minutes felt like an eternity.

When he finished, he told me to come by the next day and bring the rent money and the house would be mine. That cheered me up. The next day, I went to his house with my money in my hand ready to sign the lease, but he simply told me he was busy and asked me to return the next day. When he said it, he had a look of disdain on his face and contempt in his voice. He treated me like I was a disease, and like I was bugging him, so I left. The next day came and I went back only to receive the same response; this went on for several days until one day, I noticed another family moving into the house. Outraged, I confronted the landlord and reminded him of our agreement, but he just brushed me off like I was a nobody and walked away, offering me no explanation. I felt like I was living in the Twighlight Zone. Rage, confusion, and sadness were swirling around in my heart as I felt like a piece of trash that had been discarded. It was then that I realized I couldn't continue to live this way.

Chapter 11
He's Gone

The sixteenth birthday is a magical time in every girl's life; this is a time for proms, getting a driver's license, experiencing one's first love, and embarking upon womanhood. Sadly, this would never be me. On my sixteenth birthday, I was at my sister's house; the smell of marijuana and cigarettes filled the air. I was in her living room, which had two old black faded pieces of furniture: a love-seat and a sofa; pictures of her younger self covered its gray walls, and loud music was playing throughout the house.

My brothers and cousins were passing around a joint and a 40-ounce bottle of Olde English and reminiscing about the "good ole days." Meanwhile, in the kitchen, there were little kids scurrying around and bickering, "Give it to me! That's mine! I had it first!" Several of the adults were playing Spades while loudly talking trash about who was the best player; the others were standing around watching and talking. "I got next!" screamed one intoxicated man.

I was in the kitchen leaning against the refrigerator, having a conversation with a boy from the neighborhood. As expected, we rushed into a relationship. Once more, I thought I was in love. My son and I moved in with his sister, which was a mistake. After moving in with her, I discovered that I was not her brother's only girl—I was just one among several girls he was dealing with. I wanted to get revenge, so I started talking to another boy I knew; his name was Devonte. He was there for me in the beginning, serving as a listening ear and a shoulder to cry on. I'd turn to him whenever my boyfriend, Ray, was acting out of line. However, one night, after Ray and I had been arguing, I sought out Devonte's affection. We met at my sister's house, and what was supposed to be a night of talking and watching television turned into a night of love-making. That night was the last night I saw Devonte. Shortly thereafter, he went off to college.

I felt horrible for cheating on Ray, even though I felt like he deserved it. The following month, I was eating a pork hot-dog with mustard, ketchup, chili, and extra onions when, all of a sudden, I started to feel sick. I jumped up and attempted to rush to the bathroom, but I didn't make it in time—vomit erupted out of me like a volcano, covering my clothes. I dreaded the thought of being pregnant again. I prayed that it was just a stomach bug, but it wasn't. I had to come to terms with the fact that I was indeed pregnant. And to top it off, at the moment, Ray had gotten two other girls pregnant; this only made matters worse between us. In the days following, we spent the majority of our time arguing. The fighting got so intense his sister kicked both of us out of her house. So there I was, six months pregnant with nowhere to go. I had to go back to my sister's house, which was filled with partying, fussing, cursing, drinking, and smoking. I felt embarrassed, humiliated, and worthless again.

Playing For Keeps

July 28, 1996, is a date I will never forget. That was the day my daughter, Carly James, was born; it also happened to be the same date my first child was conceived. Carla was beautiful. She had bright grey eyes, a big round face with dimples, and sandy brown hair. She reminded me of a Cabbage Patch Doll. I just stared into her eyes and strummed my fingers across her forehead while promising her that I would always protect her from predators. I dreaded the thought of my little princess experiencing the things I did growing up. It was time for my baby and me to leave the hospital. Thankfully, my mom found another place for me, my kids, and my little brother to live. It was empty, the house had no furniture, no working appliances, and no cooling or heating system, and it was in a drug-infested neighborhood. It was easy for me to find a drug dealer who was willing to spend his fast earned money on me.

Ray was not out of the picture yet. I told him he was the father of my daughter; however, I had my doubts. After all, I remembered the night I spent with Devonte. I didn't tell Ray about that night, but Ray had heard rumors about that night, which made him question whether or not he was Carla's biological father. He immediately asked for a paternity test. And as I suspected, as the test revealed, Ray was not the father. When the results came back, Ray flew into an uproar. His eyes were red and swollen as if he had been crying for days. He began yelling at me, calling me names, and throwing objects around. I was afraid of what he might do to me next. I felt drained from the mental stress I was under. I just fell on my knees and clutched his leg while crying, and I begged him not to leave, but he left anyway. My plot of revenge backfired on me.

I called Ray several times afterwards and pleaded with him to come back to us. I told him I would do anything to make things right. He gave in and came back to us, and we became a couple again. I tried everything I could to convince him of my loyalty to him, but nothing seemed to work. Things weren't the same between us. It seemed impossible for us to rekindle the old feelings and passion we shared. But I was desperate and playing for keeps, so much so until I stopped taking my birth control pills with the hope of conceiving his child. I was determined to do whatever it took to keep him in my life.

What Else Could Go Wrong?

Whenever I found myself stressed and needed to clear my head, I'd go for a walk. I was worried about me and

Ray's relationship, whether or not we would last. While approaching the house after my long walk, I noticed a pink piece of paper on the front door. It was an eviction notice. Ray and I had ten days to vacate the property. Rather than going inside, I just sat on the front porch and contemplated what to do next.

When eviction day came, Ray and I went our separate ways; this was certainly bad timing since my mom and my little brother had moved in with my mom's new boyfriend...in another town. So I was all alone with my kids. Technically, I was still a child, but now I had adult responsibilities. One of those responsibilities was finding a place for me and my kids to live. And I chose to do just that, being willing to stoop to any level I needed to secure a place for me and my kids—even if that meant sacrificing my dignity, and my body.

Eventually, I found a house down the street. It was a large two-story multi-family unit. It was blue with burgundy steps that shook every time someone walked on them. I prayed silently every time I walked on them, asking God not to let them collapse. Another tenant already occupied the downstairs area; and to make matters worse, that tenant happened to be one of Ray's girls who he had a child with.

It didn't take long for my life to take another crazy turn. It happened again: I ended up getting pregnant again. This time, I felt numb. I was seventeen-years-old with three different children by three different daddies. Also, I had no high school diploma, no skill-set, and no job. But I couldn't simply lie down and die. I had mouths to feed. So I had to get busy trying to figure out my next step. I wanted my children to remain with me rather than get shuffled around in the foster care system, and to do this, I needed stability.

One day, I got up early and went down to the Department of Social Services and applied for public assistance. Ms. Goodhaven, the intake social worker, handed me an application after drilling me with a ton of questions: "Who is the children's father? Where do you live? How do you pay your rent? Who will give you money, and why?" I felt like I was being interrogated in a courtroom. *I see why people don't want to apply for public assistance*, I thought to myself. After hours of completing what seemed like an endless cycle of paperwork, I gave the package to Ms. Goodhaven. She took the paperwork and said abruptly, "Have a nice day. Next!" Tensions were running high in that place. Everyone seemed frustrated.

A month later, I received a notification stating I had been approved for Public Housing and welfare benefits. I was overjoyed! I packed up our belongings and moved my kids and me into the projects; this was a new experience for me. My apartment had central heating and air and working appliances. My rent was only fifty dollars a month. I was overwhelmed by a sense of peace being that I'd finally found a place to call home.

The housing complex had beautiful trees, picnic tables, and a playground area. It was a fantastic sight witnessing my children go up and down the slides, play on the swings, and fall on the ground after being getting dizzy from the merry-go-round. They were enjoying themselves. The look on their faces was priceless. It was then that I started thinking about my future. I'd never considered going back to school, but I knew I had to make a life for my children, one that would bring them happiness; and yet, I didn't know where to start or what to do. Furthermore, I didn't know anyone that could point me in the right direction.

After my kids finished playing, I gathered them up and headed back into the apartment. The whole time I was walking, I was thinking about school; I couldn't shake the thought of it. I'd never considered school as a way out before, as a way to a better life. Until that point, the only thing I thought about was survival.

On February 12th, I gave birth to my third child. There was something different about this delivery; it was a water-birth. They dimmed the lights in the room; the water was warm and soothing, and soft music was playing. The mood was perfect. I was relaxed and able to tolerate each contraction that came. I was in a squat position. When it was time to push, it felt like my bottom was about to fall out. When my baby finally came out, he surfaced in the water like he was swimming. I burst into tears. "My baby is going to drown!" I yelled. The nurses assured me that he was alright, which relieved me of my fears.

My baby had a head full of black, curly hair; big dark brown eyes that sparkled, and one adorable dimple. I knew he was special the moment I laid eyes on him. I was so happy to bring Zion home.

I'd never considered the cost of taking care of three kids. What was I going to do? I had decided I was not going back to my old ways, so I began working minimum wage jobs, sometimes two at a time. It was tiresome. The thought of school still weighed heavily on my mind, but I figured I couldn't go back to school in my present state. Anyway, I was so far behind in my schooling that the thought of obtaining a diploma and graduating seemed like a fairytale. I felt hopeless and defeated. To ease my burden, I let Zion stay with an older friend of mine who I knew was secure and trustworthy.

Things began to settle down. It was just my two oldest kids and me. I was working at a local restaurant at the time. One day, while I was walking to work, a young man named Jason approached me. He was driving a white, flashy car; he was a dark-complexioned, had deep wavy hair, chestnut brown eyes, and the cutest gap between his teeth. He was well dressed and wearing Curve cologne. He asked where I was going and if I needed a ride. Thrilled by the way he looked and what he was driving, I eagerly got into his car. He drove me to my destination. As I was getting out of the car, he pulled out a wad of cash and removed a one-hundred-dollar bill, wrote his pager number on it, and then gave it to me while telling me to page him. Upon seeing all of that money, my eyes lit up like it was Christmas. All kinds of thoughts were going through my mind. He was handsome, had money and a nice car, and he was my age. I thought I'd hit the jackpot. Things couldn't get any better. Every evening, he picked me up and took me to our favorite steakhouse for dinner. He showered my kids and me with gifts and money. I felt like I was on top of the world. However, I wondered where he was getting his money from. Later, I discovered the answer: he was a drug dealer.

You'd think that after all I'd been through I would have run for the hills once I discovered the truth about this new guy, but I didn't. I was too captivated by the money and the gifts. Both of us agreed that three children were enough, but despite our best intentions and efforts to avoid another pregnancy, I ended up getting pregnant again. This guy was livid. He then gave me an ultimatum: abort the baby or lose him. My heart dropped. *How could he say such a thing?* He wanted me to choose between my baby and having my money cut off. But there was absolutely no way I was going to "murder" my child. So I told him about my decision. Afterwards, I didn't see him around very much.

Five months into my pregnancy, he called and asked if he could come by my place. At first, I was upset with him since he abandoned me to face half of the pregnancy without him, but then I figured he wanted to reconcile. Reconciliation meant being showered again with money and expensive gifts, and I felt like I needed his support, and not just financially, but mentally and emotionally as well. My youngest son, Zion, was now back with me, so I needed all of the support I could get.

I wanted this night to be remarkable. I cooked his favorite meal: a t-bone steak, well done; a loaded baked potato, and tossed salad. I set the table for two with a bottle of sparkling grape flavored water. I placed a rose wrapped up in a note next to his plate—the note read "I love you." I put on a fitted black dress that showed my curves, a pair of red wedge heels, a dab of Curve perfume, let my hair hang down, and put on some ruby red lipstick. Then I sat, eagerly anticipating his arrival. I waited and waited and waited, but he was a no-show. I remember checking every five minutes to see if his car was pulling into the driveway, but I didn't see him. I began paging him only to get no response. Finally, I called his friend, Cedric, to see if he'd seen or heard from Jason. That's when he shared with me the terrible news. Jason was in the hospital for blunt trauma to the head. The cops were arresting him for drugs, and an altercation ensued. When I arrived at the hospital, he was barely conscious and was in handcuffs while in a wheelchair.

Several hours later, a police officer arrived and ordered me to leave the room. He informed me that Jason was under arrest and that he was about to be transported to the detention center for processing. I left the hospital feeling devastated. When I got home and opened the door to my apartment, I just stared at the extravagant table that was set for two. I then burst into tears and fell to my knees. Jason wouldn't be joining me for diner. Quite frankly, he wouldn't be joining his child and me for anything any time soon. I felt alone. "How could this be happening to me again? How can I raise four children alone?" I cried while holding my belly and weeping.

I cried myself to sleep again, just like before. But

unlike before, I was awakened by a sweet, innocent voice saying, "Mommy, get up!" My eyes popped open. For a moment, I was in a daze. As I regained consciousness, I hoped that the entire situation with Jason was only a nightmare, but I quickly realized it wasn't. That morning, I waited by the telephone for Jason's phone call. He called me and informed me of what was happening. He explained that he did not get a bond and that the State Bureau of Investigations was turning his case over to the Federal Court. When he went to trial, and the judge sentenced him to seven years in federal prison.

I didn't know what to do. The man who supported me financially was now in prison. I was now a single mother with three kids and a fourth one on the way, and I had no family around to help me, and no education. My stress level was through the roof. I was diagnosed with Toxemia, a condition characterized by hypertension; fluid retention, Oedema, and the presence of protein in the urine. I became bedridden for the remaining four months of my pregnancy.

On April 20, 2000, I gave birth to a boy, Carson. I returned to work two weeks after giving birth due to financial difficulties. I could not rest. I couldn't afford to give my body time to heal and return to normal like other new mothers. But who was I fooling? Nothing about my life was normal.

NOT JUST ANOTHER PRETTY FACE

Chapter 12
The Vision

One morning, while I was at work, the thought of returning to school came back to my mind. I tried to block it out of my head, but then I looked around at the other tired faces of my co-workers. At this point, I had a job producing Wrangler's Jeans. It suddenly dawned on me that I didn't belong there. God created me to do more than just putting buttons on a pair of jeans. God wanted more for me than sweating while working in a factory—feet hurting from standing up for long hours; fingers writhing in pain from repeatedly picking up the heavy jeans. Right then, I decided to quit my job and go back to school.

The next day, I arrived at the Family Learning Center and toured the school. It was like high school, but with a daycare. One side of the hall had a room with books, computers, a chalkboard covered with grammar, arithmetics, and fifteen adults eager to learn, and someone decorated the other side of the hall with colorful numbers (123's) and letters (ABC's). Cribs, mats, blankets, toys, cubbies, crayons, coloring books, crying babies, and running toddler running around filled those rooms.

After a thirty-minute tour of the center, Ms. Green took me into her office to explain to me the First Start Program. It was different from a traditional educational program because it provided childcare on site. Parents were allowed to bond with their children for one hour a day. During this time, parents could engage with their children by making crafts, eating lunch, coloring with them, and playing with them outside. They provided free transportation and lunch for us as we strived to obtain our General Education Diploma (or GED).

I arrived the following Monday, January 5, 2005, with a determination to graduate in May with my diploma. I shared my goal with my instructor who thought it was far-fetched, considering that I had been out of school for almost ten years with only a ninth-grade education. She gave me the pre-tests to see what books I needed to start with, and to her surprise, I scored high enough to start with the GED books. Later that day, she called me into her office and said, "Shenita, I think you are very capable of graduating with the others in May if you work hard and dedicate yourself to First Start." Her words motivated me. For once, I felt like someone truly believed in me.

For the next three months, I was determined to

beat the odds. I attended class regularly. I enjoyed the parent-child time, the parental guidance, and educational courses they provided. I was taking a test once a month, which I'd pass. I was focused, and nothing was going to stop me. May came quickly, and I only had the writing test left. Unfortunately, the school for First Start was closing on May 1st for the students in my program. They began to prepare for graduation on May 12, 2005. Ms. Green called me into her office again and asked me to close the door and take a seat. My heart was racing. I didn't know what to expect. "Miss James, I am very proud of you. You have proved yourself to be very determined and optimistic. I am doing something I have never done before. I am going to send you to Hope Filled Community College to take the writing test. Once you are finished with the test, they will email me your results. Take your time and you will do well." My heart was both relieved and thrilled. I took the pink slip she gave me and went on my way to take the test.

When I arrived, Mrs. Calya greeted me. I followed her to the testing area filled with other students, each looking as nervous as me. She gave us our final instructions and let us know when to start. When I got my paper and topic to write on, I immediately dived into; my fingers moving nearly as fast as my thoughts. I was one of the first students to complete the test. But now, I had to wait for the results. That was torture. All kind of thoughts passed through my mind: *What if I do not pass? Why did I finish before the others? Did I take my time? Should I have gone back over my work?* Mrs. Calya interrupted me. "Congratulations, Shenita! You did wonderful on your writing test! Because of your score you will receive a scholarship during your graduation ceremony." *WHAT?!!* I was in disbelief. Tears fell from my eyes. I had finally accomplished something! I dreamed about this day for over ten years but never thought it possible. Now it was happening.

At that moment, no one could convince me that I couldn't achieve my goals. No one! No longer would I walk around with my head down feeling useless. No more. I began to discover my value.

Stranger In My Bed

I started dating a guy I knew from high school named Sicon. He had a great paying job; he was nice, charming, and had a body that would make most women look twice. He loved to cook and clean. Most of all, he treated my children like they were his own. He enjoyed playing video games and preferred to be left alone. He was a home-body. The fact that he chose to spend his time at home with me and my kids melted my soul. At night, after the kids went to bed, I took off my superwoman cape, sunk into his arms, and wept while recounting the many childhood experiences I had. I looked him in the eyes and promised him that I would protect my only daughter at any cost. He seem very unemotional when I was talking to him about my past, which I didn't pay much attention to at first. However, I should have taken that as a sign.

Four years passed, and everything seemed normal; however, nothing could have prepared me for what I was about to see. One morning, I experienced what felt like an out-of-body experience. I don't know if it was, or it was merely a vision; all I knew was it felt entirely real. Sweat was pouring from my body, and I was shaking and feeling confused. These were the same feelings I got when I was at Jeffery's house as a little girl. Suddenly, in the vision or out-of-body experience, I saw a dark shadow enter into my daughter's bedroom. I snapped out of my trans and jumped out of bed, curious. I tip-toed to my daughter's bedroom, and what I saw left me speechless. I couldn't catch my breath. I felt like my heart had been ripped out of my chest by Satan himself. At that moment, my childhood flashed before my eyes. It was like I'd been transported back in time to Jeffery's house, and I saw myself lying in bed with my Punky Brewster nightgown on, and my underwear pulled down. I was there with Jeffery, trembling as he stood over me with his penis in his hands while wearing the most mischievous grin.

Suddenly, I snapped out of it and found myself back in the present moment, witnessing Sicon standing over my daughter with his pants down. He had his hands in my daughter's underwear while she lied still, frightened and pretending to be asleep. Immediately, I started screaming, "You sick bastard!!! I'm going to f**king kill you!!! Get the f**k out of my house!!!! You're going to f**king jail!!!" He froze, and before I knew it, I was beating him upside the head with my fists as he attempted to pull his pants up.

After he left, I rushed back to my daughter's room to console her. "Are you okay? What did he do? How long has he been touching you?" I asked her. Before she could answer, I fell on my knees and began to weep. I felt like I failed my daughter. Her bedroom—a room with bright colors—was now a reminder of pain and betrayal in my life. I understood the emotional pain my daughter was experiencing because I'd felt that pain every day for years.

How do I begin to pick up the broken pieces? How can I help her heal when I am wounded? Will she hate me? Will she forgive me? I sat there for a few minutes, contemplating these questions. I realized I had to get myself together and find out what happened. I asked Carly again how long this had been going on. She said, "Since I was in the fourth grade."

"Wait! What?" I needed a second to catch my breath and process what she just said. "Why didn't you tell me, Carly?" She just burst into tears. She tried to catch her breath and speak.

"Because you said if someone touched me you were going to kill them and go to jail, and I didn't want you to go to jail!"

Immediately, my mind recalled the conversation Carly and I had when she was only nine-years old. I talked to her about inappropriate touching. One morning, she was in the kitchen washing dishes, and I was in the sitting room watching Black Entertainment Television (BET). There was a song playing called "Smoking Gun" by Jadakiss featuring Jazmine Sullivan. The song goes:

CHAPTER 12: THE VISION

"Shawty is courageous, going through the stages
of where her body is more mature than her age is,
far from the daddy's little girl type.
Can't even imagine what her world is like.
It all started off as a youngin,
stepfather used to touch her and she couldn't
say nothing.
The more she held in the pain, it kept coming.
Eventually it scarred her for life as a woman,
and then he just kept touching her inside
that was crushing her.
I got something to discuss with her..."

While the song was playing, Carly stopped washing the dishes and ran into the sitting room. "That's my song," she proclaimed enthusiastically. She knew every word to the song.

As I listened closely to the lyrics, I thought, *Why would she like a song about molestation?* So I asked her, "Carly, why do you like that song so much? Has anyone touched your 'no-no' areas?"

"No, mommy. I just like that song because it's nice." Still, something didn't sit right with me, so I asked her to come and have a seat next to me on the couch.

"If anyone ever touches your 'no-no' areas, tell me. I do not care who it is. I will always believe you. I will kill someone and go to jail if anyone hurt my little princess."

"No, mommy, no one has touched me. If they do,

I will tell you."

Had I known then what I know now, I would have chosen better words to use in our little prep talk. I started to feel guilty, and even responsible for what happened to her. It was at that moment that I discovered children perceive things differently than adults. I could only imagine what my daughter was thinking. I thought about how I'd respond to her had she come forward and confessed to me that Sicon was molesting her, and I thought about how crushed I'd be had she kept it quiet. But God was looking over us. That vision or out-of-body experience was a supernatural intervention that exposed a demonic plot, a generational curse.

I told Carly I had to contact law enforcement and pursue criminal charges against Sicon. She cried hysterically, "No, mommy! No!" I was puzzled by her response.

"Why don't you want me to contact law enforcement?"

"Because all the kids at school will tease me, and it will be in the newspapers."

"Baby, they will not put your name in the paper."

"But mommy, I am your only girl! People will know who they are talking about! Mommy, please, please do not call the police! I will have to go to court and testify in front of all those people! I wish I was dead!" Right then, I ran over to Carly and hugged her with all of my might. All I could do was hold her while tears streamed down both of our faces.

What am I to do? How do I handle the guilt, shame,

and cycle of molestation? Dumbfounded, I decided not to inform law enforcement just to appease my daughter. I was afraid she'd succumb to the pressure of teasing and childhood bullying and commit suicide, but I refused to be like my mother and live in denial and allow a predator to be anywhere near my daughter. So I packed Sicon's belongings and told him never to touch or speak to my daughter again. It's important to note that this era was one where the popular expression was used: "What goes on in your house stays in your house." Looking back, I do recall reporting Jeffery to one of my teachers, who then contacted a social worker. However, they didn't call law enforcement; this was not the "Me Too" era, the era of 'See something, say something!' that we have today. There was no national outcry in society against sexual abuse, nor any advocates for the victims of sexual abuse. Carly and I would have to deal with this on our own, although at that time, neither of us knew how. We did what sexual abuse victims did at that time: block it out of our minds, moved on, and continued to live. Of course, I didn't think about the toll the trauma would have on Carly's life moving forward.

NOT JUST ANOTHER PRETTY FACE

Chapter 13

Hurt People

It was a Friday night, and my weekend had just begun. I pulled up to *The Hole In The Wall Juke Joint* in my 2001 champagne colored Honda Accord. I stepped out of the car wearing a black bodysuit that showed every curve, a red Coach pocketbook, and a pair of red patent leather three-inch heels. The smell of freshly cut grass filled the air. As I made my way to the door, a group of guys were standing around talking. I overheard someone ask, "Man, who is she? She is beautiful." I pretended not to hear their conversation. One of the guys followed me inside. "Excuse me. My name is Cypher. Can I buy you a drink?" I frowned. My first thought was, *I wish he'd go somewhere and leave me alone.* I scanned him from head to toe, starting with his feet. He was wearing a pair of chocolate Clarks Wallabee loafers, denim jeans, and a blue and white button-up long sleeve shirt. His skin was pecan brown, his face was uniquely oval-shaped, and on the left side of his cheek was a deeply indented dimple. His hair was black like charcoal with deep waves. He could tell from the look on my face that I was not interested, but I think that turned him on even more. He was determined to buy me a drink and get my number. He even followed me to the bar, still attempting to buy me a drink.

Finally, I gave in and accepted his offer to buy me a drink. After my third drink, I tried to conceal the pain I was feeling, but my emotions took over, and I sat there sobbing. Before I knew it, I was pouring out my heart to a total stranger. He placed my head on his shoulder and walked me outside to my car. He acted genuine, but I'd seen that before. He gave me his number and asked me to text him when I made it home, but I had no intention of texting or calling him.

The next morning, when I woke up, I thought about the events that transpired the previous week concerning Carly. I went into Carly's room to check on her. She was lying in her bed, texting a friend and listening to music. I asked her if she wanted to talk about what happened, and I reiterated to her that it was not her fault. She looked at me and said, "No, mommy, I do not want to talk about it. I'm okay." I kissed her on her cheek and left her alone.

I needed someone to confide in due to the agony I was feeling. With seemingly no one else to call, I gave Cypher a call. "Hello, Cypher, how are you?"

"Peace, Queen. I am good. What about you?"

"So what is up with you? I heard you are married?"

"True."

"Well, I don't want to cause any problems. To be honest, I just want to use you to get over this situation."

"You can use me. I am here if you need someone to talk to, or if you want to just get away." Never did I think this simple arrangement would turn into something that would last for years to come. Cypher was there for me mentally, even while continuing to be a husband and a father, but I began to crave more of him. I started to place a demand on his time. Pretty soon, word of our relationship got back to his wife. Of course, I denied everything. And I felt terrible, too. I knew I was wrong, but I was selfish. I was hurting and was willing to hurt someone else just to fill a void in my life. Our affair continued until his wife finally filed for a divorce. Suddenly, reality kicked in, and I realized the damage I had done to that man's home. How could I be so selfish as to hurt someone else because I was hurting? Was it because a part of me secretly envied his family relationship, which was something I yearned for? Was it because I wanted others to feel how I was feeling? At that time, I believed no one care about me. Furthermore, I didn't have much faith in anyone. I assumed everyone was hiding secrets, everyone was deceitful and putting on a front, so why should I continue to be the one getting played and used all of the time?

I should have taken some time to get healed and learn what true love is. It would have been better that I take myself out on dates rather than look for someone else to save me. I was a danger to others as well as myself. I was repeating the same bad habits while expecting different results. That's called insanity.

Although that affair was messy and built on my wounded ego, I learned several lessons from it. It led me into a state of silent reflection, where I began to take a more in-depth look at myself and my unhealed wounds. Here's a lesson to take away from my situation: You cannot heal what you conceal. Learning to love yourself unconditionally and discovering your worth are the keys to healing. When you allow the toxicity (bitterness, unforgiveness, resentment, deceit) from other people to reside inside of you, this toxicity will turn you into the very thing you hate; it will prevent you from becoming the best version of yourself.

After taking a long, hard look at myself and examining my heart, I decided that I didn't want to be the same wounded Shenita I'd been for years. I decided I wanted to be the Shenita God created me to be. I wanted to be the best version of myself. That was the declaration I needed to make to set myself in another direction.

Chapter 14
Getting Healed

Now I need to stop and inform you of something. Before you can pick up and move forward with your life after experiencing life-altering trauma and abuse, you must take the time to get healed emotionally. As I stated in the previous chapter, I'd come to a place of self-reflection where I realized I needed to get healed from the wounds of my past. I allowed my pain to mess up another man's marriage, and I realized that my pain wasn't going away on its own. I had to take a proactive step in the healing process. I had to decide that I wanted to get healed and to change. I had to declare my intentions to become a better person and then make moves in that direction. The alternative to this was to grow increasingly bitter and allow my life to dwindle away.

You might not have experienced sexual abuse at the hands of a parent or loved one like I did, but the bitterness from disappointment can and will bring your life to a halt. That bitterness can result from a divorce, infidelity, a friend or family member's betrayal, losing a job, losing a career as a result of someone else's actions, losing a loved one to tragedy and senseless violence, being picked on and bullied, experiencing domestic abuse in your relationship, or any of similar reason. The point is you must deal with the bitterness or the bitterness will deal with you.

I was bitter and didn't know it. Ironically, I was becoming the very thing I hated: a predator. I was zeroing in on wounded hearts like an animal and looking to inflict my revenge on them for the actions perpetrated on me. I was allowing my pain to make me a destructive tool in the lives of others—that's what unresolved issues and unhealed hearts will do. After seeing the ugliness of my heart, I did the one thing many people tend not to do in situations like these: I sought out professional counseling. That was one of the best things I ever did. And it wasn't a cake walk either. Counseling was hard; it forced me to face things I'd chosen to suppress. I can remember when I first met with the counselor. She was warm and inviting, but as soon as we began to get into the meet of my issues, things began to change. She had me to open up about my experiences with Jeffery, a name I didn't want to hear ever again. Until then, I was content with blocking any memory of him out of my head. Again, suppression was my tactic. Bury things. Suppress things. Try to forget things. This doesn't work; it only makes matters worse.

CHAPTER 14: GETTING HEALED

I was now confronting the horrific details of every sexual assault, and acknowledging the thoughts and emotions that accompanied them. Each time I did this, tears streamed down my eyes, and I relived every moment like I was still there. I'd be overwhelmed with the same fear, the same anxiety, the same horror, feeling of filthiness, the same confusion and anger I felt when the abuse was all happening to me as a child. That counselor took my hand and safely guided me into my past, and she did so with the intention of allowing me to look the past in the eyes and declare it doesn't define my present and my future; she wanted me to gather up the boldness to face and confront that which haunted me silently and unconsciously.

I learned that anything you don't confront will rule over your life. To gain power over an emotion or a trauma, you must confront it; this means acknowledging it, reliving it, and then addressing its root cause and true nature. During counseling, I realized that I wasn't responsible for anything another grown up did to me. I didn't cause it, invite it, or provoke it. Any and all sense of shame due to the feeling of personal blame had to be erased. I had to see the situation through fresh eyes and realize I was simply a victim of someone whose life was full of dysfunction. I also had to realize that, as a child, I wasn't in the position to protect myself, but I am in that position as an adult. I couldn't choose who I was as a child, but I can choose who I want to be as an adult. And truthfully, I can't stop what other people do to me now, but I can decide how I want to respond. People can still be mean to me today, but I don't have to internalize their actions and allow them to make me feel bad about myself and ruin my day. I can choose to acknowledge that their actions are theirs and that I am not responsible for how they act and feel; therefore, I refuse to blame myself for what they do. Maintaining my peace is my job, not someone else's.

I learned so much sitting on that therapist's couch. My life changed as a result of therapy, but it didn't end there. At the end of the day, I still had to make the decision to forgive those who hurt me and those who allowed the abuse to continue. I had a whole list of names on my forgiveness list: Jeffery, my sister, my mom, my dad, my uncle, my grandmother, Tony, Devonte, Fred, Ray, the owner of the rental property who sexually abused me, and even Sicon. One by one, I had to acknowledge their sins and transgressions against me and declare out loud that I forgive them. Of course, the forgiveness wasn't to let them off the hook for what they did; it was to free myself from their control over my mind so I could experience true freedom in my heart. I had to empty out my heart of the negative emotions I held within because of these people. Why become a toxic waste bin as a result of harboring so much negativity? Whether these people asked for it or not, I had to set my heart free, and that's exactly what I did.

A Relationship Restored

I didn't directly confront Jeffery—I didn't want to. I'd forgiven him in my heart, but forgiveness doesn't necessarily mean putting oneself in a position to be hurt and abused again. With that being said, you must forgive but you must never forget. Release what people may have done to you, but don't continue to trust untrustworthy people and put up with abuse. Take a stand! But when it comes to reconciliation, I wanted to clear the airways with my family. I wanted to rebuild the relationship with my mom most of all. Eventually, we bonded and I was able to establish the type of relationship with her I'd always wanted, the kind I needed. A relationship cannot exist without the basic elements of honesty and respect. For years, my mom lived in denial of the things her boyfriend was doing to me and my sister. She turned a blind eye and even went so far as to subject me to witchcraft just to avoid facing the truth. There was a lack of honesty in our relationship, and this led to distrust; therefore, to restore our relationship, we had to start off on the right foot.

I sat down with my mom and shared with her all of the things that happened to me. She confessed that she knew these things were happening, but felt helpless to intervene and stop them. Furthermore, she confessed that she lived with the pain and reality of what happened to me every single day; this pain ate away at her, causing her to experience sleepless nights and restlessness; it filled her with a deep sense of guilt and shame. She was still bearing this burden when I talked to her, and I felt it my obligation to help set her free. I told her I forgave her and I loved her. The look on her face set my heart at ease.

Today, my mom and I have a wonderful relationship. We talk all the time. We have become good friends. She opened up to me about some of the things she experienced in her past, and this gave me a better understanding of her as a woman. I realized that all of us were products of generations of dysfunction, that my experiences weren't unique. Through understanding, we bonded and began to help one another heal even more.

Chapter 15
Finding My Purpose

I was sitting on my balcony drinking iced tea while enjoying the smell of roses and Dogwood Blossoms and watching the bumblebees pollinate the flowers. Spring was in the air. I was reflecting on my life and thinking to myself, I wanted more for myself. But I was still unsure of how to accomplish it. I fantasized about walking across the stage of a University while wearing a gown and cap decorated with sparkling letters that read "Still I Rise," which was a quote by Maya Angelou. Around my neck, I'd have on seven honor cords representing various academic and non-academic achievements, awards, and honors. After calling my name, I'd strut across the stage showing all thirty-two teeth. The people in the crowd would be clapping and screaming, "Tina, you did it!" They'd be so loud I wouldn't be able to hear the next graduate's name being called. Of course, the depressing thought crept back into my mind: *Who am I fooling? I do not have time to go back to school! What would my major be? How would I pay to attend a university while working full time?*

I was in tug-a-war with myself. I tried making every excuse not to go back to school. The next day, while working at Tender Care Hospital, I was hanging out in the break room, enjoying my morning coffee when Mr. Bones, a doctor who worked the night shift, joined me. We knew each other outside of work. He was aware I was writing a memoir. He looked me in my eyes and said, "You know, unless you go back to school and obtain your degree, you will be nothing more than a pretty face with a story." Just then, I spit some of my coffee out of my mouth.

"What did you just say?"

"I said, unless you go back to school and obtain your degree, you will be nothing more than a pretty face with a story."

My stomach knotted up; my hands were sweaty, and my heart was racing. *How dare he say that to me?* I tried to remain calm. I did not want him to know he triggered my anxiety. "Why did you say that? I know a lot of successful writers without degrees." He then snickered.

"Oh yeah, one in how many? My colleagues will chew you up and spit you out." He then stood up and exited the break room, leaving me alone to contemplate his words. With tears in my eyes, I got up from the table and returned to work. Ironically, I was just fantasizing about walking across a graduation stage, and now, I was making excuses for not completing my education.

I felt like Mr. Bones crushed my spirit, but he didn't; he was a wake-up call. When I returned home, I started researching different schools and programs. I did not want to get a degree just to say I had a degree; I wanted a meaningful one, one that I could use. I wanted to get a degree in a field where I could help people and give hope to the broken-hearted. I decided to fill out an application online to the Green Wood University School of Social Work. I did not think I was smart enough to be accepted, but I still gave it a shot. I received an email one week later stating, "Congratulations! We are pleased to inform you that you have been accepted to Greenwood University School of Social Work." I grabbed my phone to call my friends and family and share with them the exciting news. I did not get from them the response I was expecting. I heard, "Make sure you finish." "Why social work? They don't make any money?" But I didn't care. It was my life, and I wasn't going to allow their negative responses to deter me.

It was 7:53 am, and I was hunting for a parking spot while rushing to make it to my first class on time. I was rushing to my child welfare class. When I arrived, I felt intimidated because nearly all of the students present were much younger than me. They were generally between the ages of eighteen and twenty-years-old. I sat in the back of the packed room, hoping no one would notice me. Some of the students had their cellphones in their hands, texting; others had laptops on their desks, pretending to take notes while scrolling through their

Facebook timelines. Although they seemed not to pay attention, they were technologically savvy. What took me forever to do only took them a fraction of the time to do.

I started to fall into the trap of comparing myself to them; they were young and quick-witted while I was older and not as technologically inclined. I began to lose my sense of joy and forget my purpose for being there. I was there to learn how to help people. I had to remind myself of that. Thankfully, my peers were helpful. They kept me up-to-date with technology, and I kept them on track with deadlines and assignments. Before I knew it, it was time to graduate! What was once a dream was now a reality. I recalled every negative thing the nay-sayers said about me: "You will never amount to anything! You are just a statistic! No way you will ever finish school! You are nothing more than a pretty face with a good story!" Then I thought about the fact that it's not about where you start; it's about where you end up that matters.

If you ask me how I did it, how I beat the odds and avoided being just another statistic, I will tell you I had to stop making excuses for where I was first. Secondly, I had to use my mind and figured out a way around the stumbling blocks I faced in life. Third, I had to forgive those who wronged me, including those who never acknowledged their wrongdoings. Fourth, I had to stop looking for other people to save me, and I had to save myself (with the help of God, of course). Fifth, I surrounded myself with people who were positive and who were smarter than me, people who wanted to see me exceed. They reminded me to push past my pain to keep my purpose at the forefront of my mind. Being around them reminded me that God designed me to soar in life. Lastly, and most importantly, I had to learn how to love myself unconditionally. To do this, I had to discover what the love of God is. His love is unconditional, and in it I discovered my self-worth—that my value as a woman isn't determined by who does and who doesn't like me, by what I have or don't have, by what society says about me, or any of those other factors; instead, my worth as a human being is based on the fact that I was made in the image of God, that I am a beautiful specimen because I was "wonderfully and fearfully made" by a loving God. I was able to gain freedom from the expectations of others and stop allowing others to place value on me. In fact, say that with me: "I am made in the image of God. I am loved by Him." Like David said in the Bible, "Even if my father and mother abandon me, the LORD will hold me close" (Psalm 27:10, NLT). I didn't see it then, but on those nights when I was being abused and misused and felt like I was all alone, I wasn't; God was with me, giving me a strength I didn't know I had to make it through the long night just so that I'd be in the position I am today where I am walking in a greater purpose. I learned how to turn my pain into my purpose. I discovered that the pain I endured throughout my life was designed to help others going through things they feel they can't talk about and deal with.

Childhood trauma can affect us well into adulthood. When left untreated, this trauma can lead to anxiety, depression, and many other mental health problems. These mental health problems can result in physical illnesses such as heart disease.

It can be frightening to seek out treatment for childhood trauma when you don't have the proper emotional support from friends and family, but it is necessary for your sake. Through resilience and intrepidness, I overcame my childhood trauma. During this process, I had to revisit in graphic detail some very dark places in my past. I had to relive some horrible experiences while talking to the right counselors. Furthermore, I had to accept my past for what it was and then decide not to live in it, but instead live in the present. I can't change my past, but I can decide who I want to be moving forward.

On my path to a better life, I continued to research governmental assistance programs that provided difficult educational programs. I learned more about how financial aid works in higher-level education. I put everything into improving myself, and I did it for me and no one else; this was me running full-steam into my purpose. And even as I continued on my journey, God began to speak to my heart and remind me of the things that old preacher told me back at Ms. Hope's church. I began to realize that my life—my real life—was just beginning. The journey was hard getting there, but I made it. Through prayer, I made it. On the nights when I wanted to give up, something kept pushing me forward. When it seemed as if there was no light at the end of the tunnel, I kept moving forward. And now, I saw the light. I was running for it, making a mad dash into its glorious presence.

A Dream Realized

I never imagined that what I envisioned one day while down in the dumps would manifest. There I was sitting with my blue and white cap on that was decorated with gemstones and a quote that said "God is within her, she will not fail." I was wearing a blue gown with seven honor cords around my neck while awaiting my name to be called so that I could walk across the stage and receive my degree. I graduated from college with a degree in Social Work. That was one of the happiest days of my life.

I currently serve as a social worker. My days and nights are filled with the activity of rescuing children who're trapped in abusive homes. My pain thrusts me into a purpose I didn't foresee as a child growing up. It breaks my heart to see that there are so many children who're currently experiencing the same terror I did as a child, but now I see how God shaped my life into something beautiful for His glory. For had I not gone through what I went through, I would not have had the passion to make a difference in the lives of so many others, particularly those who can't stand up for themselves—children. My pain has become my purpose, and it has created within me a passion that drives me daily. I am a difference maker. I am a world changer. I am in a blessed place in my life, experiencing a newness, a freedom and a change in mind that has allowed me to break cycles of dysfunction in my family. My breakthrough was for my children and the countless children I serve. Whereas before when I used to conceal my pain behind a smile, now my smile feels genuine, and for the first time in my life, I no longer cry myself to sleep. I sleep soundly, and peacefully.

No, my journey isn't finished—it won't be until the day I'm in the grave. Daily, I'm discovering more about myself and encountering newer and greater possibilities to make a difference in the lives of others. However, I've escaped the darkest years of my life, I made it through the darkest night, I overcame the greatest odds, and I'm here to let you know that you will make it. Take one step at a time and don't give up because a better day is coming your way. If you keep going, keep praying and asking God to be your guide, and learn to love and believe in yourself, you too will see those brighter days.

A Final Word
To Parents

Childhood sexual abuse and trauma is a reality for many children around the world. Their cries often go unheard. Many of them feel misunderstood, and their symptoms misdiagnosed. If you are a parent, you must know the signs of childhood abuse and sexual abuse. It would be best if you observed any sudden changes in your child's behavior (being withdrawn, becoming angry, violent, fearful, anxious, and other negative signs). Evaluate them; don't criticize them. Talk to them. Ask questions. Don't jump to conclusions and make sudden judgments. They are children—sometimes, they don't know how to articulate what they are feeling and what they're experiencing, so partner with them in resolving these problems as opposed to increasing their fear and anxiety by reacting defensively towards them.

About The Author

Shenita James was born on April 16, 1980, in Edenton, North Carolina. She enjoys reading, writing, and spending time with her family. Shenita is known for her encouraging words, her passion to help others, and her determination to keep going even in the face of seemingly impossible situations.

Shenita graduated from East Carolina University with a Bachelors Degree in Social Work. Shenita is employed with Child Protective Services as an investigator for children who are suspected of being abuse or neglected. She is currently pursuing her Master's Degree in Social Work in hopes of becoming a child trauma therapist.

Shenita co-authored *Healing The Little Women Inside*. She has helped many others realize that it is not where you start that determines your end, it's where you end up that counts. Hard work, dedication, determination, and putting God first is the key. Never give up, and keep your eyes on the prize.

To contact the author, go to:
www.IAmShenitaJames.com
JamesShenita@yahoo.com
Facebook: Shenita James
Instagram: Sheinta_James

CPSIA information can be obtained
at www.ICGtesting.com
Printed in the USA
LVHW091601290121
677804LV00007B/275